DETROIT PUBLIC LIBRARY

W9-CHY-426

CONELY BRANCH LIBRARY
4600 MARTIN
DETROIT, MI 48210
(313) 224-6461

JUN '05

APR 08/

Animal Rights

NOV 05

RELEASE DETROIT PUBLIC LIBRARY

$$\left[\begin{array}{c}\textbf{OPPOSING}\\ \textbf{VIEWPOINTS}^\circledR\\ \text{DIGESTS}\end{array}\right]$$

APR -- 2003

Animal Rights

JENNIFER A. HURLEY

$$\left[\begin{array}{c}\textbf{OPPOSING}\\\textbf{VIEWPOINTS}®\\\text{DIGESTS}\end{array}\right]$$

Greenhaven Press Inc., San Diego, California

No part of this book may be reproduced or used in any form or by any means, electrical, mechanical, or otherwise, including, but not limited to, photocopy, recording, or any information storage and retrieval system, without prior written permission from the publisher.

Every effort has been made to trace owners of copyrighted material.

Library of Congress Cataloging-in-Publication Data

Hurley, Jennifer A., 1973–
    Animal rights / by Jennifer A. Hurley.
        p.   cm. — (Opposing viewpoints digests)
    Includes bibliographical references and index.
    Summary: Presents opposing viewpoints about animal rights, discussing their capacity to suffer, the question of whether they can be the property of people, whether they should be used as food, and animal experimentation.
    ISBN 1-56510-868-X (pbk. : alk. paper). — ISBN 1-56510-869-8 (lib. : alk. paper)
    1. Animal rights—Juvenile literature. 2. Animal welfare—Juvenile literature. [1. Animal rights. 2. Animals—Treatment.]
I. Title. II. Series.
HV4708.H83   1999
179'.3—dc21   98-42321
                                                                                    CIP
                                                                                    AC

CONELY BRANCH

Cover Photo: Tony Stone Images/Nigel Hillier
AP/Wide World Photos: 23
Corbis: 13 (Hulton-Deutsch Collection), 17 (Charles E. Rotkin), 36 (Kennan Ward Photography), 75 (Wolfgang Kaehler)
FPG International: 25, 46
PhotoDisc: 19, 65

©1999 by Greenhaven Press, Inc.
PO Box 289009, San Diego, CA 92198-9009

Printed in the U.S.A.

CONTENTS

FOREWORD

The only way in which a human being can make some approach to knowing the whole of a subject is by hearing what can be said about it by persons of every variety of opinion and studying all modes in which it can be looked at by every character of mind. No wise man ever acquired his wisdom in any mode but this.

—John Stuart Mill

Today, young adults are inundated with a wide variety of points of view on an equally wide spectrum of subjects. Often overshadowing traditional books and newspapers as forums for these views are a host of broadcast, print, and electronic media, including television news and entertainment programs, talk shows, and commercials; radio talk shows and call-in lines; movies, home videos, and compact discs; magazines and supermarket tabloids; and the increasingly popular and influential Internet.

For teenagers, this multiplicity of sources, ideas, and opinions can be both positive and negative. On the one hand, a wealth of useful, interesting, and enlightening information is readily available virtually at their fingertips, underscoring the need for teens to recognize and consider a wide range of views besides their own. As Mark Twain put it, "It were not best that we should all think alike; it is difference of opinion that makes horse races." On the other hand, the range of opinions on a given subject is often too wide to absorb and analyze easily. Trying to keep up with, sort out, and form personal opinions from such a barrage can be daunting for anyone, let alone young people who have not yet acquired effective critical judgment skills.

Moreover, to the task of evaluating this assortment of impersonal information, many teenagers bring firsthand experience of serious and emotionally charged social and health problems, including divorce, family violence, alcoholism and drug abuse, rape, unwanted pregnancy, the spread of AIDS, and eating disorders. Teens are often forced to deal with these problems before they are capable of objective opinion based on reason and judgment. All too often, teens' response to these deep personal issues is impulsive rather than carefully considered.

Greenhaven Press's Opposing Viewpoints Digests are designed to aid in examining important current issues in a way that develops critical thinking and evaluating skills. Each book presents thought-provoking argument and stimulating debate on a single issue. By examining an issue from many different points of view, readers come to realize its complexity and acknowledge the validity of opposing opinions. This insight is especially helpful in writing reports, research papers, and persuasive essays, when students must competently address common objections and controversies related to their topic. In addition, examination of the diverse mix of opinions in each volume challenges readers to question their own strongly held opinions and assumptions. While the point of such examination is not to change readers' minds, examining views that oppose their own will certainly deepen their own knowledge of the issue and help them realize exactly why they hold the opinion they do.

The Opposing Viewpoints Digests offer a number of unique features that sharpen young readers' critical thinking and reading skills. To assure an appropriate and consistent reading level for young adults, all essays in each volume are written by a single author. Each essay heavily quotes readable primary sources that are fully cited to allow for further research and documentation. Thus, primary sources are introduced in a context to enhance comprehension.

In addition, each volume includes extensive research tools. A section containing relevant source material includes interviews, excerpts from original research, and the opinions of prominent spokespersons. A "facts about" section allows students to peruse relevant facts and statistics; these statistics are also fully cited, allowing students to question and analyze the credibility of the source. Two bibliographies, one for young adults and one listing the author's sources, are also included; both are annotated to guide student research. Finally, a comprehensive index allows students to scan and locate content efficiently.

Greenhaven's Opposing Viewpoints Digests, like Greenhaven's higher level and critically acclaimed Opposing Viewpoints Series, have been developed around the concept that an awareness and appreciation for the complexity of seemingly simple issues is particularly important in a democratic society. In a democracy, the common good is often, and very appropriately, decided by open debate of widely varying views. As one of our democracy's greatest advocates, Thomas Jefferson, observed, "Difference of opinion leads to inquiry, and inquiry to truth." It is to this principle that Opposing Viewpoints Digests are dedicated.

"Underlying all animal rights controversies—vivisection, eating meat, wearing fur, hunting, or using animals for entertainment—is a philosophical question about the relationship between people and animals."

The Changing Role of Animals in Society

Today, most people agree that causing unnecessary harm to an animal is wrong. Our laws reflect that sentiment: Neglecting a pet by depriving it of food, water, or medical attention is a misdemeanor crime penalized by costly fines or in some cases jail time. More severe forms of animal cruelty, such as torture, are considered felonies and are punishable by up to five years in jail.

The notion that animals should be protected from cruelty under the law is fairly recent. No such laws existed until the 1800s. Public displays of animal abuse were commonplace in nineteenth-century England. Carriage horses were driven until they collapsed from exhaustion; calves were packed into carts with their legs tied together; cattle and sheep were "prodded" with sharp iron hooks or whipped to death at the whim of slaughterhouse workers. Popular forms of amusement at the time included cockfighting, dogfighting, and bullbaiting—a vicious battle between a dog and a bull that often ended in a bloody death for both animals. All of these practices were perfectly legal; in fact, animal fighting was viewed as healthy entertainment.

Why did people in nineteenth-century England tolerate the blatant mistreatment of animals? Mainly it was because attitudes toward animals were different than they are today. For the most part, animals were seen as property rather than as creatures capable of experiencing pain and suffering.

Furthermore, concern about the welfare of animals was not a widely accepted view. When the House of Commons was scheduled to debate an animal protection bill that sought to abolish bullbaiting, members of Parliament considered the issue so insignificant that many failed to attend the session. The debate itself was even more fruitless. At the mere mention of the bill, the room reportedly erupted in laughter.

Although anticruelty laws proposed during the early 1800s were easily defeated, the idea that animals deserved protection from cruelty was steadily gaining support. Influenced by philosophical works such as the Reverend Humphrey Primatt's "Dissertation on the Duty of Mercy and Sin of Cruelty to Brute Animals" (1776) and John Lawrence's "A Philosophical and Practical Treatise on Horses" (1796), supporters of the humane treatment of animals began to publish their views in local newspapers. One such supporter, Richard Martin, a flamboyant and popular member of the English Parliament, was able to generate support for the cause of animals as no one else had done. A passionate advocate of animals, Martin had been so angered by an incident in which a man deliberately shot and killed his Irish wolfhound that he fought the dog's owner in a duel.

In 1821 Martin introduced a bill to Parliament aimed at preventing the cruel and improper treatment of cattle and horses. The bill was initially defeated, but upon reintroduction the following year it passed. Martin's Act was notable for two reasons: Most important, it was the first law regulating how people should treat animals. In addition, Martin's Act invigorated other legislative efforts to abolish animal cruelty. In fact, an 1829 New York State measure forbidding the malicious killing, maiming, or wounding of horses, oxen, cattle, and sheep was said to be a direct result of Martin's Act.

Two years following the passage of the Martin's Act, the Society for the Prevention of Cruelty to Animals (SPCA) was founded. The group's work had a simple but noble purpose: to make acts of animal cruelty punishable by law. In its *Annual Report*, the SPCA published lurid accounts of animal cruelty: horses beaten with pitchforks, an ox whose horns were deliberately sawed off, a stray dog that was hung from a tree and kicked to death, and a cat whose nose was bitten off by its owner. The general public responded to such testimonies with horror and indignation. Less than a decade after its inception, the SPCA had attracted a wide base of adherents, including royal patrons such as the duchess of Kent and Queen Victoria. In 1840 Queen Victoria granted the society permission to add the prefix "Royal" to its name, which made the SPCA—now called the RSPCA—a respectable, even fashionable, cause. However, despite its royal ties, the RSPCA was much more than a gentlemen's club. The organization rigorously enforced anticruelty statutes, even employing a private police force to investigate suspicions of animal cruelty and collect evidence for prosecutions. As a result of the RSPCA's activism, Martin's Act was eventually expanded to ban all types of animal fighting.

The Origins of Vivisection

Meanwhile, the use of animals in medical experiments was becoming popular among doctors and scientists. By the 1860s almost all European scientists had incorporated animal experimentation—commonly referred to as vivisection—into their research and training. Although vivisection was accepted within the medical community, the general populace, which was somewhat suspicious of medical knowledge, regarded vivisection as barbaric. Adding weight to this view was the fact that animal experiments tended to be extremely unpleasant, even grotesque. An eyewitness of Dr. Francois Magendie's experiments reported:

> I remember once, amongst other instances, the case of a poor dog, the roots of whose spinal nerves [Dr. Magendie] was about to expose. Twice did the dog, all bloody and mutilated, escape from his implacable knife; and twice did I see him put his forepaws around Magendie's neck and lick his face. I confess . . . that I could not bear this sight.[1]

Many members of the RSPCA spoke out against the practice of vivisection. Martin himself called animal experimentation "too revolting to be palliated by any excuse that Science may be enlarged or improved by so detestable a means."[2] In 1874 the RSPCA used the Martin's Act to prosecute a French physiologist and three English doctors who performed an experiment in which a dog was injected with absinthe—a poisonous liquor—to induce epilepsy. The case did not succeed in court, but the publicity it generated invoked widespread sympathy for the animals subjected to medical experiments.

During the late 1800s, however, the RSPCA's stance against vivisection began to shift. For one thing, it was not politically feasible for humane societies to counter the powerful medical establishment. The RSPCA relied on the support of its wealthy patrons, many of whom had ties to the medical community.

Furthermore, evidence of vivisection's potential benefits was mounting. In the 1850s researcher Louis Pasteur put forth the "germ theory" of disease, a theory asserting that invisible microorganisms were responsible for human illnesses. To most doctors and scientists—not to mention the general public—the notion that tiny "bugs" could infect humans was ridiculous. However, in 1876 German scientist Robert Koch presented firm evidence proving Pasteur's germ theory—proof that he had obtained by injecting mice with anthrax bacteria. Koch's findings led to improved sanitation measures, which in turn reduced the spread of disease significantly.

These developments complicated the vivisection debate. After witnessing vivisection's benefits, many people who were formerly opposed to the practice changed their views. Ultimately, the RSPCA and its sister organization, the American Society for the Prevention of Cruelty to Animals (ASPCA), took a neutral position on vivisection, refusing to condemn or defend it.

Nonetheless, vivisection still had vociferous opponents. In 1875 antivivisectionists, no longer welcome in the humane societies, began forming their own organizations, the most powerful of which were Frances Power Cobbe's Victoria Street Society and George Jesse's Society for the Total Abolition and Utter Suppression of Vivisection. Groups cropped up in the United States as well. In 1883 Caroline Earle White founded the American Antivivisection Society, which still exists today. Ironically, she could not serve as an officer of her own organization because she was a woman.

In both England and the United States, antivivisectionist groups introduced a number of bills calling for restrictions in animal research—most of which failed. Proponents of vivisection worked hard to defeat such measures; they formed lobbying forces to prevent the regulation of animal research, distributed pamphlets on the value of animal experiments, and gave testimony at legislative sessions. Opponents of vivisection, on the other hand, were far less organized and possessed limited resources compared to those of the medical community. They were unable to counter the vivisectors' most persuasive argument in favor of animal experimentation: the medical benefits gained through animal research. As a result, the antivivisection movement slowly lost its vigor. Various factors led to the movement's decline, including the death of its charismatic leaders and the onset of World War I. By the 1920s nearly all antivivisectionist sentiment had faded out.

In contrast, humane societies were still a powerful force, especially in the United States. By 1907 every state had an anticruelty statute on the books, and by 1923 anticruelty legislation had been expanded to cover a wide spectrum of issues, including

> docking horses' tails; failure to feed, water, or shelter; abandonment of decrepit or disabled animals; maliciously killing or injuring another's animal; cock fighting; prohibition of certain [hunting] traps; failure to visit traps; . . . cutting off more than a half an ear of domestic animals; cruelty [to animals] in filmmaking; and careless exposure to barbed wire.[3]

Early animal rights groups viewed the practice of animal experimentation as barbaric.

The ASPCA was instrumental in one of the most important advances for animals during the twentieth century: the passage of the 1958 Humane Slaughter Act, a law that requires meatpackers to provide animals with some form of anesthetization prior to slaughter. Before the passage of this act, animals had often experienced painful deaths. Many slaughterhouse workers left "downed" animals—those that were extremely ill or had been seriously injured in transport—to suffer a slow, agonizing death.

The ASPCA's work also led to the passage of the Animal Welfare Act, passed in 1966 and broadened in 1970, 1976, and 1985. This law, considered the most significant piece of animal protection legislation, sets a minimum standard for the treatment of animals in laboratories and by handlers, and it imposes stiff penalties on violators. The passage of laws such as the Humane Slaughter Act and the Animal Welfare Act sent an explicit message to society that the malicious treatment of animals was unacceptable and would not go unpunished.

Not Far Enough

Not everyone, however, was satisfied with the scope of such measures. The animal advocates of the 1960s and 1970s had a broader agenda: In addition to opposing animal cruelty, they also challenged accepted aspects of American life, such as hunting, wearing fur or leather, eating meat, and using animals for entertainment. New organizations—among them the Fund for Animals and the American Fund for Alternatives to Animal Research—hoped to incite "a moral revolution that would change [society's] food and clothing, . . . science and health care, [and] relationship to the natural world."[4]

This revolution, which became known as the animal rights movement, began to take shape through a series of efforts in the 1970s. In 1974 Henry Spira, a civil rights activist of the 1960s, read an article by animal rights philosopher Peter Singer in which Singer argued that animals, like humans, are capable of suffering. Just as it is immoral to inflict pain on humans, Singer claimed, it is wrong to inflict pain on animals.

Singer's philosophy inspired Spira to mobilize what was the first victorious protest of animal rights abuses. Spira's target was the New York City Museum of Natural History. Under a government grant, the museum was conducting experiments that involved blinding, deafening, and damaging the brains of cats to discover the effect on their sexual behavior. After making several unsuccessful attempts to negotiate with museum officials, Spira and his followers published reports about the experiments in local newspapers and set up pickets in front of the museum. As a result of the bad publicity, Ed Koch, the current New York congressman, toured the laboratories and spoke with the scientists in charge of the experiments. Following the tour, Congressman Koch reported:

> I said to this professor, "Now tell me, after you have taken a deranged male cat with brain lesions and you place it in a room and you find that it is going to mount a rabbit instead of a female cat, what have you got?" There was no response [from the professor]. I said, "How much has this cost the government?" She said, "$435,000."[5]

With the support of fellow congress members, Koch persuaded the National Institutes of Health (NIH) to halt funding for the project. Spira and his followers had attained what no other group had accomplished: They had not only protested objectionable research, but they had also succeeded in getting it stopped. Spira's success inspired others to organize animal rights demonstrations. Copies of Peter Singer's 1975 book *Animal Liberation* circulated among the new activists. A movement had begun.

The Silver Spring Monkeys

Dramatic cases helped catapult the movement into prominence. In 1981 Alex Pacheco, the cofounder of People for the

Ethical Treatment of Animals (PETA), volunteered to work at the Institute for Behavioral Research, an animal research facility in Silver Spring, Maryland, in order to secretly witness the conditions there. In an article published by *Animals' Agenda* in 1984, Pacheco describes what he saw while working in a lab headed by Dr. Edward Taub:

> I saw filth caked on the wires of the cages, faeces piled in the bottom of the cages, urine and rust encrusting every surface. There, amid this rotting stench, sat 16 crab-eating macaques and one rhesus monkey, their lives limited to metal boxes just 17 and ¾ inches wide. In their desperation to assuage their hunger, they were picking forlornly at scraps and fragments of broken biscuits that had fallen through the wire into the sodden accumulations in the waste collection trays below. . . . No one bothered to bandage the monkeys' injuries properly (on the few occasions where bandages were used at all), and antibiotics were administered only once; no lacerations or self-amputation injuries were ever cleaned. . . . I saw discoloured, exposed muscle tissue on their arms. Two monkeys had bones protruding through their flesh.[6]

Pacheco's vivid documentation of the facility's conditions prompted local police to seize the monkeys on the grounds of an anticruelty statute. Taub was found guilty on six counts of animal cruelty, a finding that was later overturned on the grounds that state law did not apply to federally funded research. Nonetheless, the NIH discontinued funding for Taub's laboratory.

The Vivisection Debate

Animal rights activists and researchers alike welcomed the end to Taub's experiments, which were so obviously inhumane. However, any agreement between the two groups ends there. Animal rights organizations such as PETA contend that all

At the Institute for Behavioral Research in Silver Spring, Maryland, monkeys were kept in cramped, filthy cages and denied food and medical attention.

animal research should be ended. In their view, killing animals or subjecting them to pain can never be justified—even if it has the potential to save human lives. Ingrid Newkirk, cofounder of PETA, clarifies this view: "On a moral level [using animals to meet human needs] is unacceptable because you can't justify gain based on exploitation."[7]

Those who support the use of animals in research also regard vivisection as a moral issue. Proponents of animal experimentation contend that it is unethical not to employ all possible means to save human life. According to nineteenth-century scientist and philosopher Charles Darwin, "I know that physiology cannot possibly progress except by means of experimenting on animals, and I feel with the deepest conviction that he who retards the progress of physiology commits a crime against mankind."[8]

Advocates of vivisection maintain that to reject animal research is also to reject its numerous benefits—benefits that have saved millions of human lives. The Americans for Medical Progress Educational Foundation asserts that without animal experimentation, "Polio would kill or cripple thousands of unvaccinated children and adults this year; most of the nation's one million insulin-dependent diabetics . . . would be dead; 60 million Americans would risk death from heart attack, stroke or kidney failure from lack of medication to control their high blood pressure; doctors would have no chemotherapy to save the 70% of children who now survive acute lymphocytic leukemia; [the] 7,500 newborns who contract jaundice each year would develop cerebral palsy, now preventable through photo therapy; [and] many others would join the two million already killed by [smallpox]."[9]

A Philosophical Question

Underlying all animal rights controversies—vivisection, eating meat, wearing fur, hunting, or using animals for entertainment—is a philosophical question about the relationship between people and animals. For centuries people's views on animals have been guided by the Bible's assertion that humans have complete dominion over animals. According to this view, it is perfectly acceptable to use animals for food, transport, entertainment, or to fulfill any other human needs. Of those people who agree that animals should be used as resources, most feel that animals should be protected from undue cruelty.

Animal rights advocates challenge the philosophy that people have sovereignty over animals. They maintain that animals do not exist to satisfy human needs and should therefore never be killed, held captive, or made to suffer for the benefit of

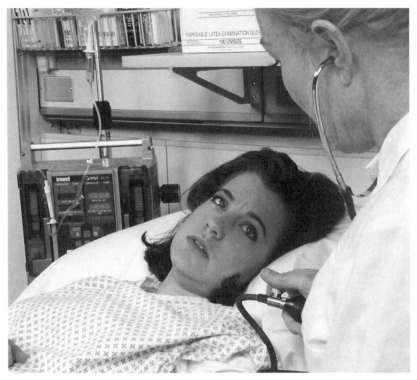

The medical progress made possible by animal testing is the main argument for continued research.

people. The most radical of these thinkers believe that keeping animals as domestic pets is exploitative because it is a form of captivity.

The fierce contention between these two groups shows no sign of abating. If anything, the animal rights debate has become more polarized in recent years. Some animal rights activists have turned to extreme measures, such as the destruction of laboratories, to get their point across. Some researchers, on the other hand, refuse to consider any restrictions on animal research. Although most Americans reject the extreme doctrines of both sides, disagreement prevails even among those whose opinions are more moderate. The essays that follow provide a context for discussing the philosophical and practical issues surrounding the question of what rights, if any, animals possess.

1. Quoted in Richard D. Ryder, *Animal Revolution*. Oxford: Basil Blackwell, 1989, p. 105.

2. Quoted in Harriet Ritvo, *The Animal Estate*. Cambridge, MA: Harvard University Press, 1987, p. 158.

3. Lawrence Finsen and Susan Finsen, *The Animal Rights Movement in America: From Compassion to Respect*. New York: Twayne, 1994, p. 52.

4. James M. Jasper and Dorothy Nelkin, *The Animal Rights Crusade: The Growth of a Moral Protest*. New York: Free Press, 1992, p. 10.

5. Quoted in Finsen and Finsen, *The Animal Rights Movement in America*, p. 61.

6. Quoted in Finsen and Finsen, *The Animal Rights Movement in America*, p. 63.

7. Quoted in David Masci, "Fighting over Animal Rights," *CQ Researcher*, August 2, 1996, p. 675.

8. Charles Darwin, *Life and Letters of Charles Darwin*. New York: BasicBooks, 1959, pp. 382–83.

9. Americans for Medical Progress Educational Foundation. On-line. Internet. Available http://www.ampef.org/research. htm.

CHAPTER 1

Do Animals Have Rights?

"If morality requires us to refrain from inflicting pain upon other people, then it should require us to refrain from inflicting pain upon animals as well."

Animals Have Rights

Animals, like humans, possess certain rights. According to the International League of the Rights of Animals, all animals are born with an equal claim on life, are entitled to respectful treatment, and have the right to live freely in their natural environment. When people eat animals, hunt them for sport, use them in medical experiments, or keep them captive in zoos, people violate the rights of animals.

Some people refuse to accept that animals have any rights at all. Animal rights opponents frequently argue that since animals do not possess the same intellectual abilities as humans— because they cannot reason, write, speak, or create art—their lives deserve less consideration than human lives. However, an increasing body of research indicates that many animals exhibit the same types of mental capabilities as humans, abilities that, according to ethics scholar Tom L. Beauchamp, include "using items such as rocks as tools, adapting to sudden changes in an environment, using intentional movements and sounds to communicate or convey feelings, and mounting novel forms of defense."[1] Furthermore, research conducted by Donald Griffin, author of the book *Animal Minds,* suggests that even a creature as seemingly unintelligent as a shrimp demonstrates the use of complex psychological tactics—including "bluffing"—

that depend on an ability to recognize other shrimp and recall previous confrontations with them.

Chimpanzees provide an excellent example of animal intelligence. The fact that chimpanzees can use tools, recognize and decode symbols, and perform tasks on command proves that the distinction between people and animals is dubious at best. As Jane Goodall notes, "Because chimpanzees show intellectual abilities once thought unique to our own species, the line between humans and the rest of the animal kingdom, once thought to be so clear, has become blurred."[2]

Clearly, animals are intelligent beings, but it is not necessary that they have intelligence in order to be worthy of

An animal rights activist stands outside Procter & Gamble to protest the company's testing methods.

rights. If a creature's moral significance depended on intelligence, then people with little potential for intelligence—brain-damaged humans, the mentally retarded, or the comatose—would not be worthy of the same consideration as fully functioning humans. Therefore, lack of intelligence cannot be used as an excuse to deny rights to animals.

The Capacity to Suffer

All human and nonhuman life, regardless of its intelligence, is unified by one important quality: Animals, like humans, possess the capacity to suffer. Despite whether animals have intellectual abilities, it is impossible to argue that animals do not feel pain; an animal in pain screams and writhes just as a human does. Ingrid Newkirk, the founder of People for the Ethical Treatment of Animals (PETA), describes this essential similarity: "When it comes to having a nervous system and the ability to feel pain, hunger, and thirst . . . a rat is a pig is a dog is a boy."[3]

The significance of pain should not be judged by the value of the sufferer—a friend, an annoying classmate, or an animal. If morality requires us to refrain from inflicting pain upon other people, then it should require us to refrain from inflicting pain upon animals as well. And, according to Richard Ryder, consultant with the Political Animal Lobby,

> We can treat different species differently, but always we should treat equal suffering equally. In the case of nonhumans, we see them mercilessly exploited in factory farms, in laboratories, and in the wild. . . . These are major abuses causing great suffering, yet they are still justified on the grounds that these [creatures] are not of the same species as ourselves.[4]

Speciesism and Racism

If we agree that it is wrong to inflict suffering upon other humans, how can we justify inflicting it upon animals? When faced with this question, opponents of animal rights claim that

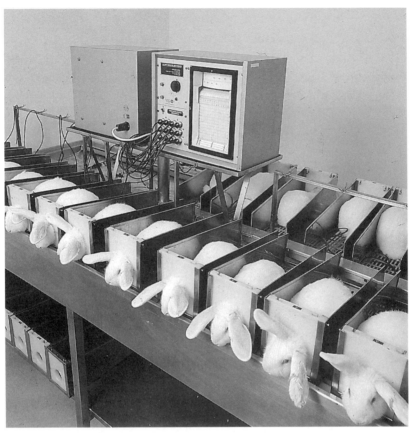

At this laboratory in Barcelona, Spain, rabbits are used to test a new drug.

humans are inherently superior to animals. This view is called "speciesism." Peter Singer, author of *Animal Liberation*, defines speciesism as "a prejudice or attitude of bias in favor of the interests of members of one's own species and against those of members of other species."[5]

Speciesists, often citing the Bible as evidence, maintain that animals exist for the sole purpose of satisfying human needs. But not only is speciesism arrogant, its logic is also disturbingly similar to the arguments used to justify racism and other forms of prejudice. The belief that humans are inherently superior to all other living things is not so different from a white supremacist's assertion that whites are a superior race and thus entitled to dominate other races.

People exploit animals for the same reason that whites kept blacks as slaves—because it benefits them. Humans have found that animals are useful; we can wear their skins, feast on their flesh, test the toxicity of our drugs on their eyes, and use parts of their bodies in our lipsticks, tires, and pills. But, as prominent author and feminist Alice Walker states, "The animals of this world exist for their own reasons. They were not made for humans any more than black people were made for whites or women for men."[6]

An Obligation to Animals

The only substantial difference between animals and humans is the ability to make ethical judgments. Animals cannot distinguish between right and wrong; humans can. Some opponents of animal rights maintain that since animals do not have the ability to make moral decisions, they do not deserve moral consideration. Actually, the reverse of this argument is true: The human capacity to act morally obligates us to prevent animal suffering. It does not give us license to cause it.

1. Tom L. Beauchamp, "Why Treat the Human Animal Differently?" *World & I*, April 1995, p. 373.

2. Jane Goodall, *Through a Window: My Thirty Years with the Chimpanzees of Gombe*. Boston: Houghton Mifflin, 1990, p. 249.

3. Quoted in Joy Williams, "The Inhumanity of the Animal People," *Harper's*, August 1997, p. 63.

4. Richard Ryder, "Toward Kinship: Speciesism and 'Painism,'" *Animals' Agenda*, January/February 1997, p. 45.

5. Peter Singer, *Animal Liberation*. New York: New York Review of Books, 1990, p. 7.

6. Quoted in Dallas Glenn, "In Defense of Animal Consciousness," *Animals' Voice Magazine*, Spring 1996, p. 32.

"Because animals do not have the capacity to act morally, much less understand the concept of morality, we cannot regard them as worthy of the same rights granted to humans."

Animals Do Not Have Rights

A woman, a boy, and a dog are on a boat in the middle of the ocean. When they begin to sink, the woman realizes that she must rid the boat of some weight. Who is tossed overboard, the dog or the boy?

Animal rights activists despise this kind of scenario because it illustrates exactly why animals do not have the same rights as humans: Animal life is simply not as valuable as human life. Even the most zealous animal rights activist would concede that it is wrong to save the dog over the boy. We may feel sorry to lose the dog, but no one can reasonably assert that the boy's life should be sacrificed in order to preserve the dog's.

Why not? Why does human life have more significance than animal life? People are more valuable than animals because a human life always has far more potential than an animal's. Even a chimpanzee, who is touted by animal rights activists as intellectually advanced, can never have a life as varied, complex, and rich as a person's. While animal life is generally confined to the business of survival, human existence is made up of endless possibilities—most of which are completely inaccessible to animals. As philosophy professor R.G. Frey states,

Part of the richness of our lives involves activities that we have in common with animals but there are as well whole dimensions to our lives—love, marriage, educating children, jobs, hobbies, sporting events, cultural pursuits, intellectual development and striving, etc.—that greatly expand our range of absorbing endeavors and so significantly deepen the texture of our lives. . . . When we look back at our lives and regret that we did not make more of them, we rarely have in mind only the kinds of activities that we share with animals; rather, we think much more in terms of precisely these other dimensions of our lives that equally go to make up a rich, full life.[1]

Human Intelligence Versus Animal Intelligence

The complexity of the human mind is what gives human life its vast potential. Human intelligence is superior to animal intelligence in a number of ways. Unlike animals, humans have the ability to communicate and record thought, generalize beyond

Reprinted by permission of Chuck Asay and Creators Syndicate.

our own experience, and make choices based on reason. The cognitive abilities of animals, on the other hand, are extremely limited. As political commentator Rush Limbaugh notes,

> Animals solve problems when they are confronted with a biological urgency of finding a way of getting what they need. But no animals sit down and ponder things and think through problems as man does. . . . Animals make sounds and communicate; but they do not communicate thought. No animal ever utters a sentence which asserts something to be true or false.[2]

While these qualities alone should be enough to establish that human life is more valuable than animal life, one exclusively human characteristic sets people distinctly apart from animals: Humans are the only living creatures who perceive the world in moral terms. Animals are entirely incapable of distinguishing between right and wrong. No animal—be it a mouse, rabbit, or chimpanzee—is able to make choices based on morality. A cat, for example, cannot choose to spare a mouse's life because it feels empathy for the creature. Because animals do not have the capacity to act morally, much less understand the concept of morality, we cannot regard them as worthy of the same rights granted to humans. Columnist Charley Reese summarizes this view: "Morality, ethics, rights and responsibilities are all human concepts and are all necessarily predicated on the ability to make choices among alternatives. If a creature lacks the ability to make a choice, then those concepts cannot apply."[3]

In fact, when left to their own means, animals tend to act viciously, often inflicting slow, painful deaths upon their prey. As Michael Sissons, writer for the *Spectator* magazine, notes, "Animals . . . are extremely violent, even to members of their own species. Every group of mammals that has ever been studied in the wild has turned out to have a murder rate greater than the worst American city—not just by a couple of orders of magnitude, but by several thousand times."[4] Clearly, animals act cruelly toward each other in the wild. In comparison, humans treat animals far more compassionately.

The Property of Humans

Sentimental animal rights activists usually take this opportunity to interject that it doesn't matter how well people treat animals, animals should not be viewed as human property. Actually, a strong case can be made that animals are the property of humans. The Bible notes this explicitly: "And God said, Let . . . [humankind] have dominion over the fish of the sea, and over the fowl of the air, and over the cattle, and over all the earth, and over every creeping thing that creepeth upon the earth."[5] Because God created animals solely for the benefit of humans, it should cause us no moral concern to use animals as we see fit.

Animal rights activists, in a desperate attempt to overcome the "cruel" laws of nature, often try to compare humankind's claim to dominion over animals with racism, asserting that the domination of people over animals is like whites' exploitation of blacks. Not only is this argument ludicrous, it is insulting to minorities to compare their struggle for rights with the quest to free rats from medical laboratories. Racism is morally wrong because race does not determine a person's worth. What animals rights activists disparage as "speciesism"—the idea that the human species has supremacy over other species— is simply a fact of nature.

Rights for Plants?

If one were to follow the logic of the antispeciesists, no living thing would be exempt from rights. As one critic of animal rights notes, "Indeed one can take this line of argument one step farther by . . . equating the struggles of minorities and women with not only the fate of animals but of plants as well, [claiming] that what is important is not that plants can think or talk, instead it is that they can die and therefore eating plants is murder."[6] Some advocates of animal rights are al-

© Tribune Media Services, Inc. All rights reserved. Reprinted with permission.

ready heading down this route; one such group suggests that cockroaches and other household pests should not be exterminated. The alternative? One should "patiently explain . . . the liabilities of their continued residence and the mutual benefits of a speedy departure."[7]

There is no end to what the animal rights activists perceive as cruel. In a society obsessed with victimhood, it is only natural that animals would emerge as the new "exploited" class.

1. Quoted in ed. Andrew Harnack, *Animal Rights: Opposing Viewpoints.* San Diego: Greenhaven Press, 1996, p. 30.

2. Rush H. Limbaugh, *The Way Things Ought to Be.* New York: Simon & Schuster, 1992, p. 105.

3. Charley Reese, "Animal Welfare vs. Animal Rights," *Conservative Chronicle,* January 24, 1996, p. 17.

4. Michael Sissons, "The Wrongs of Animal Rights," *Spectator,* September 2, 1995, p. 20.

5. Gen. 1:26.

6. James P. Skelly, "Animal Rights and Human Needs," *American Atheist,* June 1989, p. 45.

7. Lonny J. Brown, "Ethical Pest Control," *Yoga Journal,* June 1995, p. 46.

CHAPTER 2

Should Animals Be Used for Food?

"New technologies have made it possible for animals to ex-perience virtually no pain during the production process."

Human Consumption of Animals Is Not Immoral

Who can honestly resist a steak straight off the grill, a juicy piece of fried chicken, or a freshly roasted Thanksgiving turkey? Not many, according to polls on vegetarianism. A scant 1 percent of the population consider themselves to be "true" vegetarians—people who never consume meat, poultry, or fish. What's more, the Beef Industry Council reports that the consumption of meat is rising: "The number of diners in upscale steak houses grew by a quarter between 1993 and 1994. . . . Hamburger joints now get 25 percent of the restaurant business nationally. And supermarket beef sales have begun to swing back up, from a low of 65 pounds a person in 1993 to 68 pounds in 1995."[1]

Why does meat continue to be so popular, despite the trendiness of vegetarianism? The reason is simple: Meat tastes delicious. As hunter and meat eater Stephen Bodio notes, "If we weren't supposed to eat meat, why does it smell so good? Honest vegetarians I know admit they can be forced to drool by the sweet smell of roasting birds. No food known to humans smells quite as fine as any bird, skin rubbed with a clove of garlic, lightly coated with olive oil, salted, peppered, turning on a spit over a fire."[2] Let's face it: Meat is something we all crave, and there's a good reason why we do. Meat, especially beef, contains abundant quantities of protein, iron, B vitamins, and zinc—nutrients that are difficult to come by in a vegetarian diet. Some doctors advocate meatless diets, but in the next breath they're advising vegetarians to take B-12 and iron supplements in order to replace the nutrients found naturally in meat. But it's hard to see how a "healthy" diet would require supplements.

If meat provides us with essential nutrients, why is it considered unhealthy? Meat got its bad name when the medical community reported that animal fats were high in cholesterol, a substance that can clog arteries, resulting in heart disease or strokes. If meat really did cause these problems, then vegetarianism would certainly be in order. But only an *excess* of meat is unhealthy; meat consumed in moderation does not pose any health risks. Besides, cattle ranchers and meat packers are producing leaner cuts of meat, with today's average roast containing 30 percent less fat than it did a decade ago. A cut of extra-lean select beef contains a mere 4 percent of its weight in fat—enough fat to keep the juicy flavor, but not an unhealthy amount by any estimate.

Humans Are Omnivores

Even with vast evidence to the contrary, some vegetarians insist that people are not "supposed to" eat meat—a questionable claim considering the fact that humans have eaten meat for hundreds of thousands of years. Humans are omnivores, which means that our bodies are equipped to consume both meat and vegetables. Unlike species that are exclusively vegetarian, humans possess canine teeth, whose purpose is to bite into and tear flesh. Furthermore, the structure of human digestive systems proves that people are designed to be meat eaters. Because plant food is difficult to digest, herbivores—those who eat only plant food—have complex stomachs and intestinal tracts. Most importantly, herbivores have a well-developed bacteria-filled cecum, a pouch located next to the intestines that breaks down plant cells into digestible matter. If humans were meant to be vegetarian, our cecum would resemble those of other herbivores. But it doesn't. In fact, the human cecum, also called the appendix, is no bigger than a finger. It's so unnecessary to the human digestive system that it can be removed without causing any negative consequences.

Is Meat-Eating Cruel?

Vegetarians also put forth the argument that eating meat is wrong because it is cruel to animals. That's a myth, too. Yes, animals are killed for the production of meat. But do they suffer? Federal legislation requires that animals be slaughtered humanely. In accordance with these guidelines, animals are stunned so that the slaughter process is virtually painless. Furthermore, in its 1991 "Recommended Animal Handling Guidelines for Meat Packers," the American Meat Institute established even stricter guidelines for the humane treatment of slaughter animals. Those who work in meatpacking plants care about the well-being of animals and do everything in their power to minimize their discomfort. Moreover, there are economic benefits to handling animals humanely. According to the American Meat Institute,

> When an animal is stressed due to heat, anxiety, rough treatment or environmental noise, the meat that comes from the animal will be of a lesser quality. For example, if an animal becomes agitated in the chute, adrenalin is released. In cattle, this results in "dark cutters," or dark spots, in meat and an inconsistent, mushy texture. In hogs, the release of adrenalin causes Pale Soft Exudative (PSE), which appears as pale, soft spots in pork.[3]

What many vegetarians fail to realize is that the slaughtering plant is actually a far more pleasant fate for animals than the wild. As Temple Grandin, an animal lover and designer of

People in favor of using animals for food argue that animals experience a more humane death in a slaughterhouse than they do in the wild.

humane slaughtering devices, notes, "People forget that nature can be harsh. Death at the slaughter plant is quicker and less painful than death in the wild. Lions dining on the guts of a living animal is much worse. The animals we raise for food would have never lived at all if we had not raised them."[4]

1. Wendy Marston, "Beef Makes a Comeback," *Health*, November/December 1996, p. 34.

2. Stephen Bodio, "Strange Meat," *Northern Lights*, May 1996, p. 15.

3. American Meat Institute, "Just the Facts." Accessed July 17, 1998. On-line. Internet. Available http://www.meatami.org.

4. Temple Grandin, "How to Think Like an Animal," *Utne Reader*, March/April 1998, p. 47.

"Throughout their brief, sad lives, animals raised for food are subject to barbaric treatment."

Human Consumption of Animals Is Immoral

How is a living cow turned into a juicy cut of steak? Most Americans have only a dim idea of what goes on inside a slaughterhouse. The process of raising and slaughtering farm animals is so sequestered from our daily life that many people are completely unaware of its horrors. Jeremy Rifkin, author of *Beyond Beef: The Rise and Fall of the Cattle Culture*, states that "youngsters are often shocked on coming upon a beef carcass hanging in a butcher shop. They have grown up to think of meat as 'a thing,' a piece of material produced by the same processes that provide them with toys, clothes, and other such things."[1]

But meat isn't a "thing"; it is an animal who has been slaughtered, dismembered, and neatly packaged. Throughout their brief, sad lives, animals raised for food are subject to barbaric treatment—and what's more, this treatment is entirely legal. The Humane Slaughter Act, a law intended to improve conditions for slaughter animals, only protects animals from undue suffering during the actual slaughter. It does not protect them from any sort of abuse or mistreatment that occurs before slaughter.

The typical life of a veal calf illustrates the kind of misery that livestock animals experience. Separated from their mothers at birth and caged in crates so small they cannot turn around, veal calves are intentionally deprived of nutrients in order to make their meat more tender. Henry Spira of Animal Rights International describes the calves' pathetic condition: "Veal calves often cannot survive their allotted 16 weeks without drugs being pumped into them. When taken to slaughter, the veal calf is often so sick and weak that he must be dragged along the floor."[2]

The Cruelty of Chicken Farms

Some Americans have replaced their consumption of red meat with chicken because of the gross misconception that slaughtering chickens—who are "only birds," after all—is somehow more humane. However, the 7.5 billion chickens bred every year for food face more abuse than any other livestock animal; they are exempt from all provisions in the Humane Slaughter Act. Chickens are housed together in a cage so crowded that they are practically on top of each other. To prevent the chickens from eating each other—a common response to the close confines—chicks are debeaked at birth with a hot blade. Even still, cannibalism exists on a different level: Chickens are usually fed ground-up "leftover" chicken parts.

In transport from the farm to the slaughterhouse, chickens are treated roughly by handlers who are required to work at maximum speed. Paid by the chicken, these handlers grab four chickens at a time. By the time the chickens arrive at the plant, many of them suffer broken bones, injuries, and extreme discomfort from being exposed to the elements. According to one writer, "About 12.4 million chickens a year are dead on arrival at slaughtering plants due to rough handling."[3]

Next, chickens are hung upside down on a trolley line, where they are dipped headfirst into an electrified solution that stuns them before they are decapitated. The electrical stunning serves two purposes: It causes the chickens to evacuate their bowels, making for a "cleaner" carcass, and it prevents the chickens from twitching after they are decapitated.

Electrical stunning creates the illusion that chickens are being treated humanely, but in reality, stunning does little to reduce their suffering. In fact, prestunning can prolong their distress since it keeps them hanging upside down for an additional forty to sixty seconds before slaughter.

Unhealthy Diets

The operation of factory farms is especially appalling in light of the fact that meat-based diets are notoriously unhealthy. Meat is laden with cholesterol, a substance that clogs the arteries and can cause heart attacks. Moreover, according to Dr. Caldwell Esselstyn Jr. of the Cleveland Clinic Foundation, "The present American diet, with its emphasis on dairy, meat, fish, chicken and oils, accounts for 75 percent of our diseases . . . namely, heart disease; stroke; hypertension; adult-onset diabetes; obesity; breast, prostate, colon, and ovarian cancer; gout; and osteoporosis."[4]

On the other hand, nutrition experts and the United States Department of Agriculture attest that vegetarianism is a healthy diet. In addition, Oldways, a nonprofit food and nutrition education group, advocated vegetarianism in its 1997 diet standards. Of Oldways' recommended food groups, meat is conspicuously absent.

At one time, vegetarian diets were thought to be unhealthy because of the belief that only meat contained all of the essential and nonessential amino acids that make up protein. Due to this misconception, vegetarianism involved the complex task of combining certain foods in order to obtain a complete protein, one that contained both essential and

The Wizard of Id. Reprinted by permission of Johnny Hart and Creators Syndicate, Inc.

nonessential amino acids. However, the idea that vegetarians need to plan their meals carefully is a myth. According to the American Dietetic Association Journal, "Whole grains, legumes and vegetables all contain essential and nonessential amino acids. Conscious combining of these foods within a meal is unnecessary."[5] In fact, part of the reason meat-based diets are unhealthy is that they are far too rich in protein. Meat's high protein content increases the risk of kidney and liver failure, cancer, and osteoporosis.

Meat and the Environment

The consumption of meat not only harms our bodies, but it also damages the environment. According to environmentalist Howard Lyman, "Mountains of animal manure, polluted water, overgrazing, rain-forest destruction, animal suffering, human hunger, soil loss and global warming can all be attributed to the human consumption of animal products."[6] Meat consumption has a direct impact on two significant environmental problems. First, millions of acres of land are cleared or otherwise manipulated in order to raise animals for food. In South America, an estimated seventy thousand acres of rain forest is destroyed each day to provide a place for cattle to graze. The land where cattle and other animals graze inevitably becomes a wasteland that cannot sustain regrowth.

Secondly, meat production wastes resources. Animal farming requires enormous amounts of grain and cereal; the grain fed to livestock in the United States and Russia is more than the amount consumed by people in the entire Third World. According to Maneka Gandhi, former environmental minister of India, "Were all of [the grain fed to livestock] consumed directly by humans, it would nourish five times as many people as it does after being converted into meat, milk and eggs."[7] Furthermore, environmental specialists estimate that the fossil fuel energy required to produce meat is up to thirty times the amount it takes to produce grain.

Vegetarianism is much more than a culinary trend or fashionable political statement. This simple modification in our diets helps preserve the environment, curb world hunger, save animal lives, and protect our own health. With so much evidence in its favor, the only question that remains is why *not* be vegetarian?

1. Jeremy Rifkin, "The Deconstruction of Modern Meat," *Orion*, Winter 1996, p. 17.

2. Henry Spira, "Less Meat, Less Misery: Reforming Factory Farms," *Forum for Applied Research and Public Policy*, Spring 1996, p. 41.

3. Merritt Clifton, "Life on the Farm Isn't Very Laid Back," *Animal People*, October 1995, p. 8.

4. Quoted in Egypt Freeman, "The Meat of the Matter," *Health Quest*, February 28, 1995.

5. Quoted in Freeman, "The Meat of the Matter."

6. Howard Lyman, "Confessions of a 'Vegan' Cattle Rancher," *Perceptions*, March/April 1996, p. 29.

7. Maneka Gandhi, "Animal Welfare Is Human Welfare," *Resurgence*, March/April 1996, p. 18.

CHAPTER 3

Is Animal Experimentation Justified?

"Because of the medical progress made possible by animal research, we live in a world in which disease no longer threatens us at every moment, and most illnesses are completely curable."

Animal Experimentation Is Always Justified

When animal rights activists assert that animal experimentation does not save human lives, an obvious question comes to mind: Why would researchers choose to experiment on animals if it wasn't essential to medical progress? The answer is, of course, that they wouldn't. No scientist, researcher, or doctor enjoys experimenting on animals, especially if those experiments involve suffering. However, animal-based research is the only safe and effective way to develop the therapeutic drugs and medical procedures that save countless human lives. Would antivivisectionists really begrudge people their lives because a few animals had to die?

Eliminating the Plague of Polio

Animal experimentation has been the foundation for medical advances that have literally changed the world. Insulin for diabetes; organ, corneal, and bone marrow transplants; antibiotics for pneumonia; surgery for heart diseases; and the development of nonaddictive painkillers—all of these astounding medical breakthroughs were made possible through animal testing. Perhaps most significantly, the polio vaccine, given to every child in America, owes its existence to animal-based research. In the early 1950s, thousands of Americans, many of them children and young adults, were crippled or paralyzed by polio. Among the most hideous aspects of the disease was the iron lung, a huge steel breathing device that encased polio patients from the neck down. Some patients spent their entire lives inside an iron lung, with the ceiling as their only view of the world. Until the polio vaccine was introduced in 1961, parents were so afraid of their children catching the disease that "summer public beaches, playgrounds and movie theaters were places to be avoided."[1] All of this ended when a vaccine for polio was developed through experimentation on monkeys. Albert Sabin, one of the researchers who developed the vaccine, claimed that "there could have been no oral polio vaccine without the use of innumerable animals, a very large number of animals."[2] Today, animals are still needed to test the safety of each new batch of polio vaccine before it is given to children.

Animal Research and AIDS

Many researchers believe that animal-based research will eventually make acquired immunodeficiency syndrome (AIDS) as rare as polio is today. All of the treatments used to fight AIDS have been tested on animals. One experimental treatment involved the transplantation of baboon bone marrow cells into an AIDS patient. Once the transplant had been conducted, the baboon was killed painlessly with a lethal injection so that all of his tissues were available for future scientific study. Animal rights activists condemned the treatment, claiming it was wrong to kill the baboon. Would it have been right to let the AIDS patient die untreated? The sacrifice of any animal is unfortunate, but if that sacrifice saves human lives, it is completely justified. Not only do animal transplants have the potential to save AIDS patients, but they also have enormous possibilities for leukemia and lymphoma patients, who frequently go without transplants because of the lack of donors. Most importantly, almost all scientists believe that animal experiments are essential to finding an AIDS vaccine; in fact, one researcher asserts that excessively restrictive animal rights laws are the biggest obstacle to AIDS research. And, according to Joseph E. Murray, the 1990 Nobel Laureate in medicine, "Whenever a cure for AIDS is found, it will be through animal research."[3]

No Alternative to Animals

Animal rights activists sometimes contend that, since almost all disease can be effectively prevented by a healthy lifestyle, medical research is unnecessary. It would certainly be nice if this were true. Unfortunately, prevention only plays a small part in combating disease because many illnesses are either due to genetic factors or their causes remain unknown. Disease prevention can never eliminate the need for medical research, and medical research will always need animals.

The study of human cell cultures, also referred to as in vitro research, has been touted as a viable alternative to animal experimentation; after all, say animal activists, what could be a better model for humans than actual human cells? However, in vitro research has limitations. A cell culture cannot tell us the effects a drug will have on an entire human body, nor can it help doctors develop new surgical procedures. Computer-based approaches to medical research also have limitations. As David Hubel, the 1981 Nobel Prize winner in medicine states, "You can't train a heart surgeon on a computer, and to study a brain, you need a brain; a man-made machine is no substitute."[4]

In the United States, we are so accustomed to the amenities of modern medicine that we take them for granted. All of our prescription drugs, medical procedures, cosmetics, and household products have undergone animal tests to assure their safety. Because of the medical progress made possible by animal research, we live in a world in which disease no longer

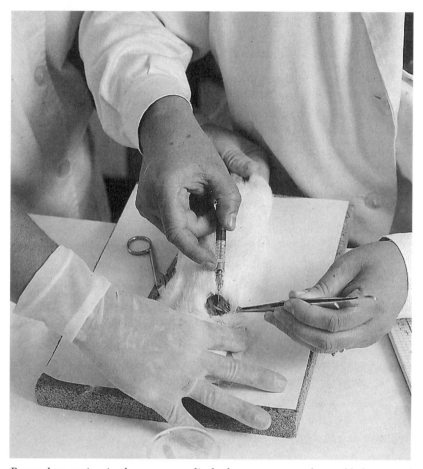

Researchers maintain that many medical advances were made possible by animal testing.

threatens us at every moment, and most illnesses are completely curable. According to the American Association for Laboratory Animal Science, "There is not a person in the United States who has not somehow benefited from the results of research involving animals."[5] Without the medical breakthroughs gained through animal experimentation, many of the animal rights activists who vehemently protest vivisection would not be around to voice their opinions. Perhaps there will be a day when medicine is so advanced that the use of animals will be superfluous; however, until every American is healthy, we cannot abandon the use of animals in research.

1. Heloisa Sabin, "Animal Research Saves Human Lives," *Wall Street Journal*, October 18, 1995, p. A18.

2. Quoted in Sabin, "Animal Research Saves Human Lives," p. A18.

3. Joseph E. Murray, "Animals Hold the Key to Saving Human Lives," *Los Angeles Times*, February 5, 1996, p. B5.

4. David Hubel, "Animal Rights Movement Threatens Progress of U.S. Medical Research," *Scientist*, November 15, 1993, p. 11.

5. American Association for Laboratory Animal Science, "Use of Animals in Biomedical Research: Understanding the Issues," undated pamphlet, p. 1.

"Unless we believe that 'might makes right,' the practice of using animals in medical research is impossible to justify."

Animal Experimentation Is Never Justified

The horrors of animal experimentation are too numerous to name: Conscious monkeys are forced to inhale toxic smoke; improperly anaesthetized dogs are subject to invasive surgery; blinded cats are dropped into vats of water; guinea pigs are coated with corrosive substances that eat through to their organs. The accounts of animal experiments surpass any horror film in terms of sheer repulsiveness.

But animal experimentation is not only grotesque, it is also wrong. Unless we believe that "might makes right," the practice of using animals in medical research is impossible to justify. Does the superior power of humans give us the right to keep animals captive and in isolation while subjecting them to painful and degrading experiments? Do we honestly believe that it is acceptable to mistreat animals for our own gain? The use of animals in experiments clearly violates animals' right to live without suffering pain or emotional distress.

Animal Experimentation Does Not Benefit People

Most Americans who favor vivisection do so because they mistakenly believe that animal experiments are essential to curing human illnesses. Animal experimentation is based on the idea that animals can be used as "models" for humans. According to Don Barnes, director of education for the National Anti-Vivisection Society, "it is simply assumed that mammalian similarities are sufficient to counteract species differences, even in the fact of significant evidence to the contrary."[1] However, animals are not simply smaller versions of humans; each animal species has a unique biological system and therefore responds differently to drugs and surgeries. Not only are animal experiments useless in the quest to combat disease, but they have also been found in some cases to actually hinder medical progress.

The reliance on animal testing to ascertain the safety of chemicals instills a false sense of confidence that the prescription drugs we take are safe. Actually, many drugs that test safe for animals are later found to cause harmful side effects in humans. One source reports that out of 198 drugs tested on animals between 1976 and 1985, 51.5 percent caused human reactions that were serious enough to warrant withdrawal from the market or substantial changes in labeling. Among

©Tribune Media Services, Inc. All rights reserved. Reprinted with permission.

Doctors Fido and Spot prepare to test a new worm medicine for harmful side effects.

these negative reactions were "heart failure, respiratory prob-lems, convulsions, kidney and liver failure, and death."[2] In ad-dition, the use of animal tests to determine a drug's safety can prevent the approval of drugs that are potentially beneficial to humans. Penicillin, for example, is fatal to guinea pigs and cats, but in humans it halts the spread of infection. Had re-searchers relied on the results from animal tests, the benefits of antibiotics—one of the most important advances in medical progress—might still remain unknown.

Animal Research and Cancer

Animal tests, commonly viewed as a miraculous research meth-od, have failed to produce any definitive advances in cancer re-search. According to Dr. Irwin D.J. Bross, director of biostatistics at the Roswell Park Memorial Institute, "Not a single new drug for the treatment of human cancer was first picked up by an animal model system. . . . The results of ani-mal model systems for drugs or other modalities have done nothing but confuse and mislead the cancer researchers who have tried to extrapolate from mice to men."[3] Many cancer researchers warn that animal tests actually impede cancer re-search. David Salzburg claims, "As long as [animal experi-mentation] is considered to be useful in detecting human carcinogens this very expensive and time-consuming procedure will continue to drain the toxicological resources of society."[4]

In many cancer experiments, researchers inject rodents with high doses of a substance to test if the substance causes cancer. The results of these tests are unreliable for two rea-sons. First, some substances that are dangerous to animals are not dangerous to humans, and vice versa. Gasoline, for exam-ple, causes kidney cancer in male rats but has no negative ef-fects on humans. On the other hand, attempts to induce lung cancer in monkeys through cigarette smoke have been largely unsuccessful.

Secondly, animal tests do little to predict whether lower dosages of the same chemicals would actually produce cancer.

In many instances, chemicals that cause cancer in high doses—aflatoxin, for example, a substance that naturally occurs in peanut butter—have no detrimental effects in low dosages. Therefore, animal-based cancer research generates fear over benign substances, yet it fails to identify truly harmful chemicals.

The Role of Animals in AIDS Research

Contrary to what many people believe, animal experimentation is not essential to productive AIDS research. Two of the most vital developments in AIDS research—the isolation of the AIDS virus and the discovery of the mechanism of AIDS transmission—involved no animal experiments. AZT, one of the first therapies available for the treatment of AIDS, was developed using human cell cultures; protease inhibitors, a more recent and effective treatment, were discovered largely because of computer technology. According to Andrew Breslin, Outreach Coordinator for *AV Magazine*, an antivivisection publication, "Virtually everything we know about HIV [the human immunodeficiency virus, which causes AIDS] and AIDS has come from non-animal methods."[5]

Some AIDS researchers have attempted to infect chimpanzees with the HIV virus because of the genetic similarities between humans and chimpanzees. However, most of the infected chimpanzees have failed to become physically ill—a clear sign that the disease works differently in animals. Funds that could be directed toward productive AIDS research are wasted purchasing, infecting, and monitoring the conditions of these isolated chimpanzees.

Medical Progress Does Not Need Animal Experimentation

History has already shown that animal experimentation is not essential to medical progress. Vital medical developments such as X rays; a vaccine against yellow fever; antidepressant and antipsychotic drugs; and surgical procedures for cardiac aneurysms, appendicitis, bladder and gall stones, brain tumors and cataracts have all been obtained through research done without the use of vivisection. Today, highly sophisticated alternatives to animal testing make the need for laboratory animals obsolete.

With the advance of biomedical research technologies, studies can now be conducted on live human cells that are cultured in petri dishes or test tubes. Using these methods, called in vitro studies, it is possible to project the effects of a chemical on the human body. In vitro tests are also more effective than animal experiments because they help us understand human reactions to diseases, not animal ones.

Virtual reality simulations have replaced the need for animals in medical training. For example, eye surgeons can now practice surgery on a three-dimensional, computer-generated image of a real eye. This simulation is a better representation of a human eye than the eye from any other species. The other advantage is that simulated surgeries can be recorded and played back, allowing surgeons to review their own performances and hone their skills.

Furthermore, three of the most prevalent medical problems in the United States—heart disease, cancer, and stroke—are almost entirely preventable. A healthy diet, regular exercise, and quitting smoking reduce the risk of these diseases to extremely low levels. While it's true that disease is never completely preventable, it is essential to stress prevention in medicine over the dubious results of animal research. The unfortunate fact about medical research is that there are few "magic cures."

The reason why animal experimentation is such a contentious issue is that people tend to view it as a decision between saving animals and saving people. However, this is not the case. There are numerous viable alternatives to animal experimentation. It is time to demand an end to a practice that is both medically and morally unsound.

1. Don Barnes, "Vivisection: A Window to the Dark Ages of Science," *Animals' Agenda*, July/August 1996, p. 21.

2. Peggy Carlson, "Whose Health Is It, Anyway?" *Animals' Agenda*, November/December 1996, p. 19.

3. Quoted in National Anti-Vivisection Society, "The Truth About Cancer Research," *Expressions 2*, 1994, p. 22.

4. Quoted in Aaron Wildavsky, "Regulation of Carcinogens: Are Animal Tests a Sound Foundation?" *Independent Review*, Spring 1996, p. 45.

5. Andrew Breslin, "Non-Animal Methods Triumph in AIDS Research," *Anti-Vivisection Magazine*, Spring 1997, p. 2.

"While animal-based research may sometimes be necessary to save human lives, animals should not be used in any experiment that fails to show a direct correlation between animal-based research and lifesaving medical progress."

Animal Experimentation Is Sometimes Justified

The controversy surrounding animal experimentation is often vicious, with each side stubbornly clinging to its ideology. Provivisectionists believe that animals should always be sacrificed for human gain, while antivivisectionists contend that animals should never be sacrificed for human gain. The most reasonable position on animal experimentation, however, lies somewhere in the middle. While animal-based research may sometimes be necessary to save human lives, animals should not be used in any experiment that fails to show a direct correlation between animal-based research and lifesaving medical progress.

When animals are used in experiments, conditions should be such that the animals are free from physical and psychological suffering. Currently, not enough steps are taken to ensure the welfare of laboratory animals. The standards are easily sidestepped, and many of them seem arbitrary. For example, dogs are required to be given daily exercise, a benefit that is not extended to other animals. Laboratories must take steps to account for the psychological well-being of chimpanzees, but not cats or rabbits. Regardless of cost, high standards for the treatment of all laboratory animals is in order. If the use of animals is so essential to medical progress, then scientists and researchers should not mind the added cost and effort of treating those animals with kindness.

Cruel, Useless Tests

Unfortunately, a number of animal tests currently conducted in laboratories have no obvious medical benefits and cause considerable suffering to animals. Maternal deprivation experiments are the most horrific. In these studies, young primates are separated from their mothers in order to determine the effects of maternal deprivation. In some cases, the primates' real mothers are substituted with "monster mothers"— terry-clothed surrogates that cannot hold or comfort the infant. The results of these experiments are no surprise: The primates experience severe psychological distress when deprived of their mothers. Examples of their distress include "young animals in slouched postures crying out for their mothers, socially withdrawn, shaking and clasping themselves, or sometimes huddled in the fetal position in a corner of their cages."[1] Experiments such as these tell researchers nothing new—it has already been widely established that primates are extremely social animals who crave maternal attention. However, maternal deprivation studies continue to be conducted under the auspices that they provide "insight" into maternal deprivation of humans. If researchers are interested in studying maternal deprivation in humans, there is no lack of real-life human subjects. Maternal deprivation experiments on primates are simply cruel and unnecessary.

Another animal experiment that should be abolished is the LD-50 test, which stands for Lethal Dose 50 percent. This refers to the amount of a substance that will kill half of a test group of animals when the substance is forcibly ingested or inhaled by an animal. LD-50 tests are conducted to measure the toxicity of certain ingredients based on their effect on live animals. Since the test cannot reliably predict how humans will react to the substance, they are of little use. The test, which was developed in the 1920s, is outdated, useless, and horribly cruel. The large doses of drugs given to these animals inevitably result in terrible suffering, including "pain, convulsions, discharge, diarrhea and bleeding from the eyes and mouth."[2]

The Draize test has similar effects. This test, which determines the toxicity of cosmetics, detergents, and other household substances by applying them to the eyes of rabbits, no longer serves any purpose. Due to previous animal experiments and other forms of testing, the toxicity of nearly all chemicals is already known. Therefore, these tests only confirm—at a high price to animals—what researchers already know.

New Cancer Research

Demanding the end to cruel and unnecessary experiments, however, does not mean that animal experimentation does not have a place in medical research. One can be concerned about the welfare of laboratory animals yet support their use when no sufficient alternative exists. Unfortunately, animal studies are sometimes the most effective means to test new drugs and surgeries. In the quest to find treatments for the most debilitating human diseases—including AIDS and cancer—no avenue of research should remain unexplored.

In the case of cancer, animal research has produced significant developments. In 1960 researcher Judah Folkman discovered something important about cancer through animal tests: From his observation of tumors in animals, Folkman learned that tumor cells secrete a substance that causes blood vessels to sprout tiny capillaries. Without the production of these capillaries, however, tumor cells cannot grow. This knowledge led researchers to search for substances—called angiogenesis inhibitors—that would shut down blood vessel growth.

By 1996 doctors in Folkman's laboratory had discovered two angiogenesis inhibitors—angiostatin and endostatin. In November 1997, Folkman and his colleagues reported that endostatin had significantly shrunk human cancers that had been grafted onto mice. The substance has not yet been tested on humans, but scientists predict that angiogenesis inhibitors have enormous potential for cancer treatment, either alone or in combination with existing treatments.

The cancer research conducted by Folkman and his colleagues illustrates the proper place for animal testing in medicine. Folkman's animal experiments demonstrate a clear relationship between animal studies and significant medical progress. Put in perspective, the sacrifice of these mice to cancer research could mean saving the lives of cancer patients worldwide. Currently, the prognosis for these patients is not good. According to writers Geoffrey Cowley and Adam Rogers, "Only half of all cancer patients survive five years."[3]

Since the relationship between animal experimentation and medical progress is not always clear-cut, deciding what animal experiments are truly necessary is not a simple task. The difficulty of establishing guidelines, however, should not prevent reforming the way animals are used in medical research. In Britain, laws require researchers and scientists to justify their use of animals in experiments. Such a measure, if implemented worldwide, would be a small but significant step toward the conscionable use of animals in medical research.

1. Lawrence Carter-Long, "Life Without Mother," *Mainstream*, Winter 1997, p. 19.

2. National Anti-Vivisection Society, "The Ugly Side of the Beauty Business," *Expressions 2*, 1994, p. 11.

3. Geoffrey Cowley and Adam Rogers, "Of Mice and Men," *Newsweek*, May 18, 1998, p. 58.

CHAPTER 4

Should Wildlife
Be Protected?

"Hunting is about pure conquest: the triumph of man over less powerful creatures."

Hunting Is Unconscionable

For centuries, hunting has been portrayed as a test of honor, bravery, and manhood. It is often viewed as a competition between two worthy opponents—a courageous hunter against an elusive, crafty prey. Hunting, however, is not a harmless "sport." An examination of current hunting practices shows that hunting inflicts serious pain on animals.

Bears suffer some of the most despicable treatment by hunters. Because bears are evasive prey, hunters have developed methods that ensure a kill. In "hounding," a hunter releases a pack of dogs to chase a bear up a tree, where escape is impossible. Another method, "baiting," refers to the practice of luring bears to a particular spot with barrels of pastries, fish, or animal carcasses. Because these methods allow the bear no chance of escaping, they make the hunter's success inevitable. Although some states have outlawed hounding and baiting, others are dominated by fierce prohunting groups that refuse to ban any hunting practices for fear that hunting will be phased out entirely.

Furbearing animals such as mink, foxes, coyotes, and martens are also victims of vicious hunting practices. Since their size and speed makes them difficult to shoot, these animals are usually lured into traps. The most commonly used trap, the leghold trap, is designed to hold an animal in place until the trapper arrives and "humanely" kills it. However, in a desperate struggle to free themselves, many animals severely injure themselves, sometimes chewing off their own limbs in order to escape. Hunters claim that the traps restrain animals painlessly, but residents who live near trapping areas often report the sounds of animals screaming in pain.

> Trapped animals unable to free themselves face the threat of freezing to death, dying from thirst or starvation, or being attacked, while helpless, by predators, until the trapper arrives to dispatch them, often by primitive and barbaric means such as clubbing, strangulation, or stomping them to death. Animals such as beavers, who are victims of water-set traps, can take as long as twenty minutes to drown.[1]

The other commonly used trap is a conibear, or "instant kill" trap, a device with baited prongs that are designed to snap shut on an animal's spinal column at the base of the skull. This trap is promoted by some hunters as more "humane" because it instantly kills the animal; however, when the bars miss their target location—as they frequently do since the trap requires that the animal be a specific size—the animal is left to suffer a prolonged death. Studies have shown that conibear traps "kill less that 15% of trapped animals quickly, and more than 40% usually die slow, painful deaths as their abdomens, heads, or other body parts are squeezed between the trap bars."[2]

The Unconquerable Hunter

Current hunting practices not only inflict pain on animals but also give hunters an unfair advantage. With their arsenal of traps, devices, and weapons, hunters are virtually unbeatable against wild animals. Hunting methods have grown increasingly elaborate and foolproof. According to one writer, "Hunters

now have access to gadgets that boost their abilities consider-
ably, such as night-vision scopes (used to sight game after
dark), headphones that amplify sound, infra-red sensors (used
to track game) and radio collars for dogs, which alert hunters
to the location of their prey."[3]

But perhaps the sickest form of hunting is the canned hunt,
sometimes referred to as "caged kills." In a caged kill, hunters
pay large sums of money—sometimes thousands of dollars—
for hunts that are essentially staged. Exotic animals, most of
them domesticated from living in zoos, are brought to a clear-
ing and released as prey for the hunters. Since most of these
animals have lost their survival instinct, they are no match for
the hunters and are killed easily. Caged hunts are the epitome
of trophy hunting: the pitiful practice of mounting and displaying the heads of killed animals to gain respect among
other hunters.

In an attempt to portray hunting as ethical, hunters often
claim that they abhor methods of hunting that place animals
at a disadvantage, maintaining that they always seek a "fair
chase." Yet hunting by definition is unfair. Even when a hunter does not track an animal by helicopter, shine lights in deer's
eyes to stun them, bait animals with food, or use computer devices to determine their location, he still has an advantage
over animals because he possesses a gun. The gun assures the
hunter that he risks no harm from the animal. His life is never
threatened, even when he is pursuing an animal that is potentially dangerous. The game most commonly stalked by hunters, however, is extremely docile: deer, elk, duck, beaver, and
mink. In light of this fact, how can hunters honestly portray
hunting as "competition"? In truth, hunting is about pure
conquest: the triumph of man over less powerful creatures.

The desire for conquest, however, comes with a steep price.
In order to facilitate hunting, state agencies burn forests, build
roads through wild areas, and pour millions of dollars into the
law enforcement of game regulations and hunter education.
Hunting has contributed to the extinction of species such as the

passenger pigeon and the heath hen, and it has led to the endangerment of the bison, the grizzly bear, and many others. A long history of hunting in the United States has upset the natural food chain, harmed the environment, and wiped out animal species. It is time for hunting's path of destruction to end.

1. "Fact Sheet: What's Wrong with Trapping?" *Trans-Species Unlimited,* undated pamphlet.

2. Camilla Fox, "What Trappers Won't Tell You," *Mainstream,* Fall 1997, p. 19.

3. "Hunting Restrictions," *Issues and Controversies On File,* February 7, 1997, p. 60.

"If you contribute in any way to the killing of animals—whether it is by eating meat, wearing leather shoes, or purchasing products that have been tested on animals—it is completely illogical to oppose hunting."

Hunting Is Not Unconscionable

Most of us are familiar with the stereotype of the hunter: bloodthirsty and ignorant, with a gun in one hand and a beer in the other. Like most stereotypes, however, this representation is unfair. As hunter Ryland Loos notes, "For every mud-splattered pickup with guns displayed in the rear window and boisterous, camo clad, knife-carrying drivers, there is a car or two with hunting gear and coveralls stowed out of sight in the trunk, driven by someone whose greatest fall enthusiasm you would never suspect. Hunters . . . run the gamut of personality types."[1] Among hunters you'll find nature lovers, businessmen, artists, and housewives. Every hunter has a different reason for hunting, but nearly all of them will tell you that what they kill, they eat—very few people hunt for the sole purpose of recreation.

Unfortunately, hunting is currently being threatened by groups who believe that one of the oldest American traditions is "cruel." This view is sheer hypocrisy. Every year, billions of animals die in order to satisfy the needs of humans, yet some of the same people who contribute to animal slaughter on a daily basis are outraged over the "barbaric" practice of hunting. According to hunting advocate Gene Mueller:

The very people who want to outlaw hunting because they say it is cruel, frequently are the same people who enjoy dining on fattened calves, preferring,
however, to call the baby cows veal. Either way, the
subject is quickly changed when they're reminded
that in order for a little cow to be converted to veal
it has to be whacked over the head with a hammer.[2]

The fact is, if you contribute in any way to the killing of
animals—whether it is by eating meat, wearing leather shoes,
or purchasing products that have been tested on animals—it is
completely illogical to oppose hunting. It makes no sense to
approve of one type of killing and condemn another.

Cute Animals Versus Ugly Ones

Most opponents of hunting, for all their ranting about animal
"rights," don't really care about animals; they care about
"cute" animals. Opponents of hunting are always outraged
over the hunting of animals they consider cute: beaver, bear,
duck—and particularly deer, which remind people of Bambi.
Animals that fall outside this category, such as cows and chickens, are fair game for slaughter. Ugly animals are a different
matter altogether. As hunter Gail Collins puts it, "Most people would happily wipe out a family of rats with an Uzi. Give
a deer fangs and scales, and you would have mobs of torch-
bearing citizens marching on town halls across the nation, demanding their extermination."[3]

Hunters, on the other hand, are committed to the preservation of wildlife—all wildlife. In fact, the licensing fees for
hunting pay for most conservation efforts. If it weren't for
hunters, many wildlife conservation programs would quickly
go bankrupt. According to Terry McDonell, editor and publisher of *Sports Afield* magazine, "Each day, through license
revenues, excise taxes and other income sources like Duck
Stamps, sportsmen contribute $3 million to wildlife conserva-
tion efforts—more than $1 billion a year."[4]

Too Many Deer

As legislators rush to enact antihunting laws, they disregard hunting's important function as a wildlife management tool. Hunting bans have dire consequences, especially for areas with exploding deer populations. Today, the U.S. deer population exceeds 18 million. Most of these deer have invaded the suburbs outside of New York, Washington, D.C., and other eastern cities. Deer are drawn to these areas by the golf courses, landscaping, and gardens—all of which make for delicious food. The presence of so many deer, at one time merely a nuisance, is now hazardous to humans.

Deer often dart out into oncoming traffic in the middle of the night, giving drivers no chance to swerve or stop. The deer almost always die in these collisions, and the drivers often suffer serious injuries. In New York State alone it is estimated that deer are responsible for fifty thousand car accidents a year. Furthermore, deer carry ticks that cause Lyme disease in humans—a disease that can be debilitating, even fatal, to children, the elderly, or the sick.

Due to restrictions on hunting, the deer population has exploded. Deer cause major traffic accidents and devour expensive landscaping.

The overpopulation of deer is not only a threat to humans but also a danger to the deer themselves. The deer who are not maimed or killed in car accidents often starve or freeze to death in the wild. Other deer suffer a more terrifying fate: Coyotes and dogs have been known to eat the flesh of a still-living deer.

A Predatory World

It is difficult to accept that we live in a predatory world. All of the earth's animals are either predators, prey, or both. Nature dictates that animals are human prey. People often confuse the violence inherent in predation with cruelty; however, the relationship between the predator and its prey is often one of respect and reverence. Philosophy professor Ann S. Causey best describes the complex relationship between the hunter and its prey:

> Hunting is one of the few activities that allows an individual to participate directly in the life and death cycles on which all natural systems depend. . . . An ethical relationship with wildlife relies on an appreciation of ecosystems, of natural processes. Such an appreciation is gained through familiarity, over time, with effort, curiosity, humility, and respect. These are the lessons that hunting teaches.[5]

1. Ryland Loos, "Friends of the Hunted," *Conservationist*, November 1993, p. 104.

2. Gene Mueller, "Why Modern Men (and, Increasingly, Women) Hunt," *Washington Times*, September 20, 1996, p. G6.

3. Gail Collins, "Cook the Geese: A Good Word for Bambi-Bashing," *New York Times*, October 6, 1996, p. E14.

4. Terry McDonell, "Hunters Are Not Gun Nuts," *New York Times*, June 3, 1995, p. 19.

5. Ann S. Causey, "What's the Problem with Hunting?" *Orion*, Winter 1996, p. 27.

"If zoos were really committed to preserving endangered species, their money would be much better spent helping protect natural habitats instead of keeping wild animals captive outside their natural environment."

Zoos Harm Animals

From the outside, zoos and aquariums appear to be a haven for wild animals, a place where they are protected, cared for, and admired. Unfortunately, the sad truth about zoos is that they harm animals more than help them. The only real purpose zoos serve is to entertain people.

If you examine an animal in captivity, its restlessness and boredom are obvious. Confined in cramped areas, zoo animals do not have the freedom of movement that they need. A dolphin in the ocean, for example, travels fifty miles a day—the equivalent of five hundred laps around a typical marine park pool. According to animal advocate Jeffrey Moussaief Masson, "[Dolphins and whales] are animals that normally have the entire ocean at their disposal, and to confine them [in marine parks] is, basically, to put them in prison."[1] The same is true for land animals, most of whom are accustomed to running great distances. Not only are captive animals deprived of exercise, but they are also denied their natural habitat, which is full of smells, sounds, foliage, and other animals. Even the most "natural" zoo exhibits—which usually contain little more than a few logs and a patch of grass—fail to provide the most important element of nature: Zoo animals do not hunt for their food. Writer Jared Diamond summarizes how this affects animals' lives:

In the wild, animals spend most of their time on food: searching for it, capturing it, processing it, and eating it, often in many small amounts at many different places. . . . In zoos, though, food traditionally consists of prepared chow that requires no capturing or processing, placed in a pan that requires no finding, and provided once a day. The animal gobbles down the chow in 5 minutes, leaving it 23 hours and 55 minutes a day to be bored.[2]

Lessons Learned from Zoos

Because zoo animals cannot take part in the activities that would normally occupy them—hunting for food, exercising, and socializing with other animals—they spend their time

Reproduced from *The Spectator* with permission.

pacing back and forth or they develop abnormal behaviors such as "vomiting and reswallowing their food (as captive gorillas often do), eating their feces, being abnormally aggressive, or grooming themselves far more than any wild animal would."[3] The animal behaviors that people observe when they visit a zoo are the behaviors of a captive animal, not a wild one. That's why zoos are not educational. As one source says, "The major lesson learned from zoos seems to be that people still view animals as a form of entertainment, not as individuals who deserve the chance to live natural lives in their native habitats."[4]

Zoo enthusiasts will often defend zoos on the grounds that they help protect endangered species. Most animals kept in zoos or aquariums, however, are not endangered. In fact, some endangered species are rejected because they are not "cute" enough to draw crowds. When nonendangered species breed, "surplus" animals are often sold to medical laboratories, where they are used in experiments, or to traveling circuses. Animals who end up in circuses suffer a worse fate than those in zoos; they are usually confined in windowless trucks unless they are performing. Animal trainers use sharp metal rods to "coax" circus animals into doing tricks. Elephants in particular suffer when sold to circuses: Due to the stress of living inside small, unventilated trailers, many of them die or attempt to escape during performances.

Do Captive Breeding Programs Benefit Endangered Species?

Zoos often keep endangered species in captive breeding programs, which are designed to help species develop a stable population that can be returned to the wild. This endeavor sounds noble, but every time the zoo captures a young animal for "preservation" purposes, up to ten adult animals may be killed due to their attempts to defend the young animal. Furthermore, animals bred in captivity do not have a great chance of survival. According to Zoo Check, an organization that argues against the use of zoos in conservation, as many black rhinos in zoo-based captive breeding programs die as are bred. Animals who do survive captive breeding are often unequipped to deal with the challenges of the wild. Releasing captive animals back into the wild has such little chance of success and is so costly that most zoos do not even attempt it.

Preserving Natural Habitats

If zoos were really committed to preserving endangered species, their money would be much better spent helping protect natural habitats instead of keeping wild animals captive outside their natural environment. Zoos often spend millions of dollars on flashy new exhibits meant to attract more visitors; however, the same amount of money could be spent preserving habitats so that animals could survive in the wild. As columnist Christine Bertelson notes,

> For $200 an acre, the zoo could buy shoes, uniforms, Jeeps and tracking equipment to keep poachers from killing black rhinos and elephants vanishing from parks and preserves in Africa. . . . Or, for a mere $17.5 million, the zoo could completely underwrite the World Wildlife Fund's project to conserve the biodiversity of Russia, including threatened giant sponges, Siberian tigers and sea eagles.[5]

The only reason zoos choose not to spend their money on preserving natural habitats is to preserve their own existence. Zoos, above all, are financial institutions. Because many zoos are competing with other entertainment industries such as amusement parks, they funnel money into exhibits that will attract the most visitors—not exhibits that will best benefit animals. The notion that zoos are educational is a false illusion. Zoos and marine parks are just sad examples of people exploiting animals for their own entertainment.

1. Quoted in Karen Singer, "The Inner Life of Animals," *E: the Environmental Magazine*, September/October 1995, p. 35.

2. Jared Diamond, "Playing God at the Zoo," *Discover*, March 1995, p. 83.

3. Diamond, "Playing God at the Zoo," p. 83.

4. People for the Ethical Treatment of Animals, "Zoos: Pitiful Prisons." Accessed July 16, 1998. On-line. Internet. Available http://www.peta-online.org/facts.

5. Christine Bertelson, "With $40 Million, Zoo Should Save the Real Thing," *St. Louis Post-Dispatch*, November 16, 1995, p. 1B.

"Because zoos inspire appreciation for animals, they are the most effective way to motivate people to work for environmental change and the preservation of endangered species."

Zoos Can Benefit Wild Animals

Since the beginning of the century, zoos have been vital to the preservation of endangered species. Without zoos, the Mongolian wild horse, the European bison, and the American bison—species that were once nearly obsolete—would remain only as a part of history. These and hundreds of other endangered species have been literally brought back to life by the work of zoos. With an estimated nine hundred species in serious danger of extinction over the next century, the animal kingdom is facing a crisis that only zoos can avert. According to Dan Wharton, director of the Wildlife Conservation Society's Central Park Wildlife Center in New York City, "Zoos worldwide have assumed a critical role in preserving . . . diversity. Pressed by the current environmental crisis, modern zoos have become a kind of Noah's Ark to ensure, through captive breeding, survival of a few of the most endangered vertebrate species now perishing in a sea of extinctions."[1]

How can a species that has been virtually wiped out be restored? Zoos commonly respond to such a crisis with captive breeding programs. In these programs, a few of the last remaining animals of a species are brought to a zoo, where they are bred in a safe, captive environment until their population is large and stable enough to reintroduce into the wild. According to one source, "Captive breeding of an endangered species can make the difference between its success or failure."[2] Captive breeding programs have consistently achieved their goal of preserving and regenerating species. The black-footed ferret, the cheetah, the Wyoming toad, and the peregrine falcon all risked extinction until captive breeding efforts raised their populations to a stable level. In 1975, before captive breeding programs were instituted to save the peregrine falcon, only 39 pairs of the falcon were in existence in North America. Captive breeding helped bring the number of falcons up to 994 pairs, all of which have been released into the wild. A similar program restored the black-footed ferret, whose numbers were down to a startling 18 in 1985. Now, thanks to captive breeding, there are 300 ferrets in captivity as well as a large surplus that is reintroduced into the wild each year.

Despite the overwhelming success of captive breeding, opponents of zoos insist that the money used to fund captive breeding programs would be better spent on preserving animal habitats. However, since of the goal of captive breeding is to restore animals to the wild, captive breeding programs are often implemented in conjunction with efforts to prevent habitat destruction. Unfortunately, many of the habitats that once housed millions of animals are already completely destroyed. Although it is possible to rebuild lost habitats, zoos act as a refuge for animals until natural habitats are regenerated—a process that can take hundreds of years.

The New Zoos

For animals who have either lost their habitat or risk extinction, zoos provide an environment that closely resembles the wild but is safe. Whereas early zoos are known for their cramped, spare cages, contemporary zoos reproduce natural habitats as accurately as possible. As writer Charles Hirshberg notes, "Zoos are being reinvented, revolutionized. Old cages are being knocked down and replaced with lush habitats."[3] Increasingly, zoo habitats are spacious, outdoor areas replete with trees, grass, and ponds. Recent technology allows zoos to even supply the exact smells and sounds that animals encounter in nature. According to one proponent of zoos, "The trend is toward displaying biologically sound groups of different animals in large settings with facilities for their recreation and comfort. Zoos provide healthful, natural diets and tend to create natural habitats that are no longer always available 'out there' in the real world."[4] The Wild Animal Park in San Diego, California, is the epitome of the new zoo. At the park, animals roam freely in a large field and are undisturbed by visitors, who caravan around the field's perimeter. These zoo animals have all the amenities of the wild: food, freedom of movement, natural terrain, and interaction with other animals.

Inspiring Environmentalism

Without zoos, most people would never have the opportunity to witness and understand the beautiful creatures that inhabit our world. Zoos provide the public and researchers with information about animals' biological characteristics, habits, and species.

Biological education is good for its own sake, but it also benefits both animals and the environment. Because zoos inspire appreciation for animals, they are the most effective way to motivate people to work for environmental change and the preservation of endangered species. As Michael H. Robinson, director of the National Zoological Park in Washington, D.C., states, "Zoos . . . are, potentially if not often actually, a powerful vehicle for biological education. Here people can be moved by the wonder and glory of real living things to act to save ecosystems, rather than species."[5] When people have firsthand experience with endangered animals, they are more inclined to

Many believe that zoos increase environmental awareness by allowing people to witness the world's fascinating creatures.

dedicate their time, money, and support to causes that benefit endangered species and the environment as a whole. Zoos are responsible for much of the passion people feel about protecting animals and the environment.

1. Dan Wharton, "Zoo Breeding Efforts: An Ark of Survival?" *Forum for Applied Research and Public Policy,* Spring 1995, p. 92.

2. Julianne Couch and Tracey Rembert, "Back from the Brink," *E: the Environmental Magazine,* July/August 1996, p. 23.

3. Charles Hirshberg, "Miracle Babies," *Life,* March 1997, p. 30.

4. Tom Brakefield, "A Short History of Zoos," *Lamp,* Winter 1995/1996, p. 16.

5. Michael H. Robinson, "Beyond the Ark," *Issues in Science and Technology,* Spring 1993, p. 85.

APPENDIX A

Related Documents

Document 1: The Animal Welfare Act

The Animal Welfare Act, passed by Congress in 1966, was designed to protect animals from cruelty and neglect. In the following excerpt, the United States Department of Agriculture's Animal and Plant Health Inspection Service discusses the act's provisions and the methods by which these provisions are enforced.

The Animal Welfare Act

Since 1966, the U.S. Department of Agriculture (USDA) has enforced the Animal Welfare Act (AWA) to protect certain animals from inhumane treatment and neglect. Congress passed the AWA in 1966 and strengthened the law through amendments in 1970, 1976, 1985, and 1990. The USDA's Animal and Plant Health Inspection Service (APHIS) administers the AWA, its standards, and its regulations.

The Law

The AWA requires that minimum standards of care and treatment be provided for certain animals bred for commercial sale, used in research, transported commercially, or exhibited to the public. Individuals who operate facilities in these categories must provide their animals with adequate care and treatment in the areas of housing, handling, sanitation, nutrition, water, veterinary care, and protection from extreme weather and temperatures. Although Federal requirements establish acceptable standards, they are not ideal. Regulated businesses are encouraged to exceed the specified minimum standards.

Exemptions

The AWA regulates the care and treatment of warm-blooded animals, except those, such as farm animals, used for food, fiber, or other agricultural purposes. Currently, cold-blooded animals, such as snakes and alligators, are exempt from coverage under the Act. Retail pet shops are not covered under the Act unless the shop sells exotic or zoo animals or sells animals to regulated businesses. Animal shelters and pounds are regulated if they sell dogs or cats to dealers. Pets owned by private citizens are not regulated.

Pet Protection

To help prevent trade in lost or stolen animals, regulated businesses are required to keep accurate records of acquisition and disposition and a description of the animals that come into their possession. Animal dealers also must hold the animals that they acquire for a period of 5 to 10 days to verify their origin and allow pet owners an opportunity to locate a missing pet.

Animal Fighting

The AWA prohibits staged dogfights, bear or raccoon baiting, and similar animal fighting ventures.

Licensing and Registration

The AWA also requires that all individuals or businesses dealing with animals covered under the law must be licensed or registered with APHIS.

Research Facilities

In addition to providing the required standards of veterinary care and animal husbandry, regulated research facilities must provide dogs with the opportunity for exercise and promote the psychological well-being of primates used in laboratories. Researchers must also give regulated animals anesthesia or pain-relieving medication to minimize the pain or distress caused by research if the experiment allows. The AWA also forbids the unnecessary duplication of a specific experiment using regulated animals. Research facilities must establish an institutional animal care and use committee to oversee the use of animals in experiments. This committee is responsible for ensuring that the facility remains in compliance with the AWA and for providing documentation of all areas of compliance to APHIS. The committee must be composed of at least three members, including one veterinarian and one person who is not affiliated with the facility in any way. The AWA also does not permit APHIS to interfere with research procedures or experimentation. Regulated research facilities include hospitals, colleges and universities, diagnostic laboratories, and many private firms in the pharmaceutical and biotechnology industries.

United States Department of Agriculture, Animal and Plant Health Inspection Service, APHIS Fact Sheet, March 1995.

Document 2: The Universal Declaration of the Rights of Animals

In September 1977 the International League for Animal Rights and affiliated national leagues met in London for the Third International Meeting on the Rights of Animals. At this meeting, activists created the Universal Declaration of the Rights of Animals, a document explicating the rights of animals. The following section, excerpted from Michael W. Fox's book Animals Have Rights, Too, *consists of the document's final text, which was submitted, along with a petition signed by over 2 million people, to the United Nations Educational, Scientific, and Cultural Organization (UNESCO) and the United Nations Organization (UNO).*

Preamble

Whereas all animals have rights,

Whereas disregard and contempt for the rights of animals have resulted and continue to result in crimes by man against nature and against animals,

Whereas recognition by the human species is the foundation of the coexistence of species throughout the animal world,

Whereas genocide has been perpetrated by man on animals and the threat of genocide continues,

Whereas respect for animals is lined to the respect of man for men,

Whereas from childhood man should be taught to observe, understand, respect, and love animals,

It Is Hereby Proclaimed:

Article 1.

All animals are born with an equal claim on life and the same rights to existence.

Article 2.

i. All animals are entitled to respect.

ii. Man as an animal species shall not arrogate to himself the right to exterminate or inhumanely exploit other animals. It is his duty to use his knowledge for the welfare of animals.

iii. All animals have the right to the attention, care and protection of man.

Article 3.

i. No animal shall be ill-treated or be subject to cruel acts.

ii. If an animal has to be killed, this must be instantaneous and without distress.

Article 4.

i. All wild animals have the right to liberty in their natural environment, whether land, air or water, and should be allowed to procreate.

ii. Deprivation of freedom, even for educational purposes, is an infringement of this right.

Article 5.

i. Animals of species living traditionally in a human environment have the right to live and grow at the rhythm and under the conditions of life and freedom peculiar to their species.

ii. Any interference by man with this rhythm or these conditions for purposes of gain is an infringement of this right.

Article 6.

i. All companion animals have the right to complete their natural life span.

ii. Abandonment of an animal is a cruel and degrading act.

Article 7.

All working animals are entitled to a reasonable limitation of the duration and intensity of their work, to necessary nourishment and to rest.

Article 8.

i. Animal experimentation involving physical or psychological suffering is incompatible with the rights of animals, whether it be for scientific, medical, commercial, or any other form of research.

ii. Replacement methods must be used and developed.

Article 9.

Where animals are used in the food industry they shall be reared, transported, lairaged, and killed without the infliction of suffering.

Article 10.

i. No animal shall be exploited for the amusement of man.

ii. Exhibitions and spectacles involving animals are incompatible with their dignity.

Article 11.

Any act involving the wanton killing of an animal is biocide, that is, a crime against life.

Article 12.

i. Any act involving the mass killing of wild animals is genocide, that is, a crime against the species.

ii. Pollution or destruction of the natural environment leads to genocide.

Article 13.

i. Dead animals shall be treated with respect.

ii. Scenes of violence involving animals shall be banned from cinema and television, except for humane education.

Article 14.

i. Representatives of movements that defend animals' rights should have an effective voice at all levels of government.

ii. The rights of animals, like human rights, should enjoy the protection of law.

Michael W. Fox, *Animals Have Rights, Too.* New York: Continuum, 1991.

Document 3: Types of Contemporary Animal Protectionists

Those in favor of increased protection for animals differ widely in their strategies, goals, and ideological beliefs about the rights of animals. The following chart, which appears in James M. Jasper and Dorothy Nelkin's book The Animal Rights Crusade: The Growth of a Moral Protest, *explains the key differences among three groups of animal protectionists: welfarists, pragmatists, and fundamentalists.*

	Beliefs About Animals	Major Goals	Primary Strategies
Welfarists	Objects of compassion, deserving of protection. Clear boundaries between species.	Avoid cruelty; limit unwanted animal populations.	Protective legislation, humane education, shelters.
Pragmatists	Deserve moral consideration; balance between human and animal interests. Some hierarchy of animals.	Eliminate all unnecessary suffering; reduce, refine, and replace uses of animals.	Public protests, but pragmatic cooperation, negotiation, and acceptance of short-term compromises.
Fundamentalists	Have absolute moral rights to full lives without human interference. Equal rights across many species.	Total and immediate elimination of all animal exploitation.	Moralist rhetoric and condemnation. Direct action and civil disobedience. Animal sanctuaries.

James M. Jasper and Dorothy Nelkin, *The Animal Rights Crusade: The Growth of a Moral Protest.* New York: The Free Press, 1992.

Document 4: Beef and Animal Suffering

Proponents of vegetarianism believe that the mass production of meat causes animals to suffer. The Spiritual Realization Institute, a religious organization that advocates vegetarianism, contends in the following section that the methods of raising, transporting, and slaughtering cattle are cruel.

Cattle are exposed to harsh conditions, rough handling, and often outright abuse and cruelty throughout their short lives.

- Cattle are routinely castrated, dehorned, and hot-iron branded without anesthesia. These procedures are performed solely for the economic benefit and convenience of beef producers.
- Cattle endure extreme weather conditions from blizzards to drought when foraging on the open range. Many animals suffer and die from freezing, thirst, starvation, untreated disease, predation, and poisoning by toxic plants.
- After several months on the range, cattle are transported to feedlots where they are fattened on grain. There are 42,000 feedlots in 13 states. The largest 200 of them feed nearly half the cattle in the United States. In a typical feedlot, tens of thousands of animals are crowded into muddy, fly-infested, manure filled areas where stress makes them susceptible to shipping fever and other painful debilitating diseases.
- Because cattle aren't physiologically suited to consume large amounts of grain, the abrupt change in diet from grass to grain causes many painful digestive problems. The most common of these is rumenitis-liver abscess complex, which affects approximately 8 percent of all grain-fed cattle.
- Fending off flies can cause cattle to lose half a pound a day, so beef producers regularly spray feedlot cattle with highly toxic insecticides.
- To increase weight gain and reduce costs, some feedlots have begun experimenting by adding cardboard, newspaper, sawdust and even cement dust to feed. Others add chicken and pig manure or industrial sewage and oils.
- When feedlot cattle reach 1,100 pounds, they are trucked to slaughterhouses. Transported animals are often handled brutally, shocked with electric prods, beaten, kicked, and dragged. They may be deprived of food and water and suffer extremes of weather for long periods. Livestock trucks are frequently overcrowded and result in falls, tramplings, and suffering from injuries during transportation.
- "Downers," animals who suffer broken legs, pelvises, necks, or backs or who otherwise can't walk off the trucks, are not humanely euthanized. Instead, they are routinely chained by the neck or a leg and dragged out of trucks and onto the killing floor where, often in agonizing pain, they may wait hours to be slaughtered.
- Animals who are too sick to be slaughtered are not euthanized. Instead, they may be thrown onto the "dead pile" and left to die from disease, thirst, starvation, or hypothermia.

- Even today, the slaughter process remains primitive and violent. Animals enter the killing floor one-by-one. Each is stunned by a pneumatic gun and, as it sinks to its knees, a chain is hooked onto a rear hoof, mechanically hoisting the animal overhead. Workers with long knives then slit each animal's throat, severing the jugular vein and carotid artery, leaving the animal to bleed to death hanging upside down.
- Although stunning prior to slaughter is required under the Federal Humane Slaughter Act of 1958 and 1978 (except for kosher and other religious slaughter), in actuality, stunning isn't always successfully accomplished due to incompetence, indifference, or faulty equipment.
- Kosher slaughter is particularly cruel because the animals are not stunned. Fully conscious and terrified, they are hoisted upside down by one leg to await slaughter.
- More than 100,000 cattle are slaughtered every twenty-four hours in the United States.
- The average American eats seven 1,100-pound steers in his or her lifetime.
- Veal calves are among the most inhumanely treated farm animals. They are taken from their mothers at birth to spend their entire lives chained at the neck and isolated in narrow indoor wooden stalls (called "crates") designed to limit movement. Lack of exercise and a liquid diet of milk-substitute, which is deliberately iron-deficient, slow muscle development to create pale, tender ("white") meat. Veal calves frequently become anemic, often suffering from chronic diarrhea and weakness. Many die before slaughter.
- Animals used for food and fiber are specifically exempted from anticruelty laws in many states. In other states, routine beef industry practices—such as castration without anesthesia and dragging "downers" to the slaughterhouse killing floors are either implicitly not covered by anticruelty laws or not enforced. Prosecutors in cattle-producing states rarely bring cruelty charges against beef producers.
- In many states, if a beef producer treated his dog the way he routinely treats his cattle, he would likely be arrested, tried, fined and/or imprisoned, and his dog would be confiscated.
- There are only two federal laws that cover farm animals: the Humane Slaughter Act and the Twenty-Eight Hour Law, which pertains only to the approximately 5 percent of animals who are transported by rail and over water. This law requires that animals be given rest, food, and water if they are in transit for more than twenty-eight hours.
- There is no federal law to ensure that farm animals have proper care, suitable living conditions, or protection from abuse and cruelty. The federal Animal Welfare Act doesn't protect animals used for food and fiber except when such animals are used in biomedical and other laboratory experiments.

The Spiritual Realization Institute, "The Real Cost of Beef," http://www.neonblue.com/sri/suffer.htm.

Document 5: Humane Methods of Slaughter

The Humane Slaughter Act of 1978 prescribes standards for the handling and slaughtering of animals. In the following excerpt, the American Meat Institute summarizes the act's requirements, discusses the economic and ethical benefits of humane slaughter, and describes new methods of humane slaughter.

Meat packers are bound legally and compelled ethically and economically to handle livestock in the most humane manner possible.

The Humane Slaughter Act of 1978 dictates strict animal handling and slaughtering standards for packing plants. Those standards are monitored by some 8,000 federal meat inspectors nationwide:

- The Act specifies that animals must be handled and moved through chutes and pens in ways that do not cause stress.
- Livestock must be rendered insensible to pain prior to slaughter. The Act details the methods that must be used to stun animals.
- The Act requires that animals have access to water and that those kept longer than 24 hours have access to feed.
- Animals kept in pens overnight must be permitted plenty of room to lie down.
- The Act also forbids the dragging of downers or crippled livestock in the stockyards, crowd pen or stunning chute. . . .

The Ethical and Economic Reasons to Treat Animals Humanely

There are those who would argue that the terms "humane slaughter" are contradictory terms. Arguing the use of animals for food is a philosophical debate that likely will never be resolved to everyone's satisfaction. The fact is, meat and poultry have been staples of our diet since the beginning of time.

Many religious laws from different faiths have formed the basis for modern slaughter practices. One common theme among all faiths has been a respect for animals, avoidance of animal suffering and appreciation for the nourishment that they provide. These themes permeate the practices of the meat packing industry.

Regardless of their religious backgrounds, those who work in packing plants are comfortable around animals and have concern for their well-being. The sound of an animal in distress is unmistakable and disturbing. Plant workers take pride in caring for the animals that come into their plants and ensuring that discomfort is minimized and that the slaughter process is as painless as it can be. When the slaughter process is performed correctly, the process is so rapid that livestock never feel pain. Research continues to identify new ways to improve the slaughter process and enhance humane practices. These developments are embraced by the meat industry.

Economic Benefits of Humane Slaughter

In addition to a natural, human concern for animals, there are distinct economic benefits that result from humane handling.

When an animal is stressed due to heat, anxiety, rough treatment or environmental noise, the meat that comes from the animal will be of a lesser quality. For example, if an animal becomes agitated in the chute, adrenaline is released. In cattle, this results in "dark cutters," or dark spots, in meat and an inconsistent, mushy texture. In hogs, the release of adrenaline causes Pale Soft Exudative (PSE) tissue, which appears as pale, soft spots in pork.

In addition, animals that are calm and well-handled will walk through the chutes to be slaughtered and will enable the process to operate efficiently. A stressed animal may buck and attempt to get out of the chute. This causes other animals to become agitated, and often the production line must be stopped. It is in a plant's interest to ensure that this does not happen.

Even back on the farm, there is an incentive to treat animals humanely. For example, the use of electric prods causes breeding sows to fear people. Australian research has shown that sows that are fearful of people will farrow fewer piglets. Therefore, farmers who treat their livestock humanely will benefit from a higher yield.

Clearly, the best choice, the economically sound choice, is the humane choice.

New Developments in Humane Handling
When an animal remains calm during the slaughter process, it produces a better product. Minimizing the excitability and stress of an animal can be accomplished through proper handling practices and facility design and maintenance.

A number of innovations have been made in plants that contribute to humane handling of animals. Some are very technical and scientific. Others are rooted in good common sense. Many of the ideas have been generated by the research of Temple Grandin, Ph.D., assistant professor at Colorado State University. Grandin's research has involved walking through cattle chutes and processing lines and into cattle and hog restrainers to observe the process from the point of view of the livestock. Through this research, Grandin has found that excitability often can be minimized with very minor changes to the facility or handling practices.

Following are examples of techniques that can be used to improve handling:

- **Use of Spray Mists**—It has been proven that hogs . . . that are lightly misted as they wait in pens are soothed and relaxed. Typically, hogs will exert the characteristic behavior of huddling together and on top of one another when misted. Such behavior indicates that they are not stressed.

- **Reduction of Noise**—High-frequency sounds or loud intermittent noises are likely to cause animals to "balk" or become stressed and agitated. Cattle often balk at high-pitched noises, such as the whine of undersized hydraulic plumbing, but ignore a low frequency rumbling sound, like that of a conveyor belt. The sound of metal clanging and banging or hissing air often startles cattle. Tightening up loose metal and piping hissing air outside by using a muffler can make a dramatic difference in the stress levels of cattle.

- **Elimination of Distractions**—Wiggling chains that hang down may frighten an animal. Anything that creates a "sparkle" or reflective effect also can frighten animals. Securing chains or other dangling ropes and wires can reduce stress.
- **Improved Ventilation**—Smells blowing into the faces of approaching livestock from a stunning box or restrainer will cause animals to balk and refuse to enter. Ventilation problems can ruin the performance of the best systems, according to Grandin. It is important that a ventilation system suck smells away from approaching cattle.
- **Use of Effective Lighting**—Both cattle and hogs tend to move from darker places to brighter areas. To attract the animals, light must be aimed in the direction the animals are travelling—not at them, which would impede movement. When lighting is done correctly, animals move through the chute calmly and efficiently.
- **Removal of Impediments**—A piece of paper lying in a chute will cause hogs and cattle to freeze in their tracks. Plants now understand that by removing anything, no matter how small, that does not belong in the chute, they can keep livestock moving along without the need to prod them.
- **Painting Facility Single Color**—Cattle and hogs are sensitive to changes in color and texture of floors and fences. Painting facilities a single color improves movement dramatically and keeps the line of livestock moving without interference.
- **Use of Proper Restrainers**—Animals must be restrained during the slaughter process. When done right, a restrainer will have a calming, soothing effect on animals. A proper restrainer applies some pressure to the sides of an animal, but not enough to cause discomfort. Restrainers that use slow, steady motions, as opposed to jerky ones, also result in better handling. A "low-stress" restraint also requires solid sides and barriers around the cattle to prevent them from seeing people.

American Meat Institute, "Humane Slaughter Act and Voluntary Industry Guidelines," http://www. meatami.org/FactWL01.HTM.

Document 6: Medical Advances Made Using Animals

People who support the use of animals in research contend that animal experimentation advances medical progress. The following is a list of medical gains achieved through animal experiments, as cited by the American Medical Association.

Pre-1900	• Treatment of rabies, anthrax, beriberi (thiamine deficiency) and smallpox
	• Principles of infection control and pain relief
	• Management of heart failure
Early 1900s	• Treatment of histamine shock, pellagra (niacin deficiency) and rickets (Vitamin D deficiency)
	• Electrocardiography and cardiac catheterization

1920s   • Discovery of thyroxin
            • Intravenous feeding
            • Discovery of insulin—diabetes control
1930s   • Therapeutic use of sulfa drugs
            • Prevention of tetanus
            • Development of anticoagulants, modern anesthesia and neuromuscular blocking agents
1940s   • Treatment of rheumatoid arthritis and whooping cough
            • Therapeutic use of antibiotics, such as penicillin, aureomycin and streptomycin
            • Discovery of Rh factor
            • Treatment of leprosy
            • Prevention of diphtheria
1950s   • Prevention of poliomyelitis
            • Development of cancer chemotherapy
            • Open-heart surgery and cardiac pacemaker
1960s   • Prevention of rubella
            • Corneal transplant and coronary bypass surgery
            • Therapeutic use of cortisone
            • Development of radioimmunoassay for the measurement of minute quantities of antibodies, hormones and other substances in the body
1970s   • Prevention of measles
            • Modern treatment of coronary insufficiency
            • Heart transplant
            • Development of non-addictive painkillers
1980s   • Use of cyclosporin and other anti-rejection drugs
            • Artificial heart transplantation
            • Identification of psychophysiological factors in depression, anxiety and phobias
            • Development of monoclonal antibodies for treating disease

Quoted in Andrew Harnack, ed., *Animal Rights: Opposing Viewpoints.* San Diego: Greenhaven Press, 1996, p. 78.

Document 7: Alternatives to Animal Experimentation

The People for the Ethical Treatment of Animals (PETA) and other animal rights groups maintain that there are viable alternatives to the use of animals in research. The following section, excerpted from a PETA fact sheet on animal experimentation, describes existing alternatives to animal tests conducted by the cosmetic industry and medical researchers.

Alternatives to animal tests are efficient and reliable, both for cosmetics and household product tests and for "medical research." In most cases, non-animal methods take less time to complete, cost only a fraction of what the animal experiments they replace cost, and are not plagued with species differences that make extrapolation difficult or impossible.

Products Without Pain

Avon Products, Inc., which until June of 1989 killed about 24,000 animals a year to test its products, now uses many non-animal tests, including the Eytex method. Eytex, developed by InVitro International in Irvine, Calif., assesses irritancy with a protein alteration system. A vegetable protein from the jack bean mimics the cornea's reaction when exposed to foreign matter. The greater the irritation, the more opaque the solution becomes. The Skintex formula, also developed by InVitro International, is made from the yellowish meat of the pumpkin rind; it mimics the reaction of human skin to foreign substances. Both Eytex and Skintex can be used to determine the toxicity of more than 5,000 different materials.

In the Neutral Red Bioassay, a product of Clonetics Corporation in San Diego, Calif., a water-soluble dye is added to normal human skin cells in a tissue culture plate with 96 "wells." A computer measures the degree to which the dye is absorbed by the cells, indicating relative toxicity and eliminating the observer bias, one of the factors that limits the effectiveness of tests on animals. EpiPack, also made by Clonetics, is the first commercial product to contain live, normal cloned human cells, which are exposed to test substances in various dilutions.

Tissue and cell cultures can be grown in the laboratory from single cells from human or animal tissues. Three companies have developed artificial "human" skin which can be used in skin grafts for burn victims and other patients and can replace animals in product tests.

Marrow-Tech, headquartered in La Jolla, Calif., makes NeoDerm, which begins with the injection of skin cells into a sterile plastic bag containing a biodegradable mesh. The cells attach to the mesh and grow around it, like a vine on a garden lattice. After the segment of skin is sewn onto the patient, the mesh gradually dissolves. Biosurface Technology, of Cambridge, Mass., uses the patient's own cells to grow a skin to replace the epidermis (the top layer). Organogenesis Inc., also of Cambridge, has found customers for its Testskin in Avon, Amway, Estee Lauder, and other leading cosmetics companies.

The CAM Test uses fertilized chicken eggs to assess eye irritancy by showing the reaction of the chorioallantoic membrane to test substances. Because this membrane has no nerve fibers, the test causes no discomfort or pain. This test is intended for use by cosmetics and household product manufacturers, but egg membranes have also been used to culture viruses and vaccines. (Although we should strive to use no animals or animal byproducts in experiments, egg membranes are preferable to sentient animals.)

Medical Applications

In medicine, perhaps the most informative research takes place not in test tubes, but in hospitals and clinics and the offices of statisticians and epidemiologists. Clinical surveys, using human volunteers, case studies, autopsy reports, and statistical analyses, permit far more accurate observation and use of actual environmental factors related to human disease than is possible with animals confined in laboratories, who contract diseases in conditions vastly different from the situations that confront humans. Long before the famous smoking beagle experiments began, statisticians and epidemiologists knew that cigarette smoking causes cancer in humans, yet programs to warn people about the hazards of smoking were delayed while more animal tests were carried out to the satisfaction of the tobacco industries, and proved "inconclusive."

Mathematical and computer models, based on physical and chemical structures and properties of a substance, can be used to make predictions about the toxicity of a substance. TOPKAT, a software package distributed by Health Designs Inc., predicts oral toxicity and skin and eye irritation. It is "intended to be used as a personal tool by toxicologists, pharmacologists, synthetic and medicinal chemists, regulators, and industrial hygienists, among others," according to HDI. It is used by the Food and Drug Administration, the Environmental Protection Agency, and the U.S. Army.

The Ames test involves mixing the test chemical with a bacterial culture of Salmonella typhimurium and adding activating enzymes to the mixture. It was able to detect 156 out of 174 (90 percent) animal carcinogens and 96 out of 108 (88 percent) non-carcinogens.

The Agarose Diffusion Method was designed in the early 1960s to determine the toxicity of plastics and other synthetic materials used in medical devices such as heart valves, intravenous lines, and artificial joints. In this test, human cells and a small amount of test material are placed in a flask, separated by a thin layer of agarose, a derivative of the seaweed agar. If the test material is an irritant, a zone of killed cells appears around the substance.

People for the Ethical Treatment of Animals Factsheet: Alternatives: Testing Without Torture.

Document 8: Historical Experiments on Monkeys

One of the most controversial issues in animal experimentation concerns the use of primates in medical research. In the following excerpt from The Monkey Wars, *author Deborah Blum gives an account of the gruesome experiments performed on monkeys during the 1950s through the 1970s.*

In a 1957 experiment, scientists plunged unanesthetized rats into boiling water in order to measure blood changes; in 1960, scientists wanting to study muscle atrophy immobilized the hind legs of cats with steel pins for 101 days, until the tissues withered. In 1961, researchers studied the effect of microwave blasts on dogs. Their detailed records noted that the unanesthetized animals began to pant rapidly as radiation increased, that their tongues swelled, that their skin crisped, and that if their body temperature was allowed to climb beyond 107 degrees Fahrenheit, the dogs died.

For that matter, monkeys didn't fare so well. They were heavily used by the military to test the effects of bomb-level radiation. In 1957, 58 rhesus macaques were put inside tubes set near the drop point—Ground Zero—for a nuclear bomb test. To no one's surprise, those set in tubes along the flashpoint of the explosion were fried. Still, those tests bred others. During the 1960s and 1970s, approximately 3,000 monkeys were exposed to up to 200 times the lethal dose of radiation, put on treadmills, forced to keep moving through electric shock, and measured for endurance. Army reports describe the monkeys as going into convulsions, stumbling, falling, vomiting, twisting in an apparently endless and futile search for a comfortable position. Researchers have shot rhesus macaques in the head with rifles, the barrel of the gun held just an inch from their skulls; shot them in the stomach with a cannon impactor accelerated to 70 miles an hour to study blunt abdominal trauma. Monkeys have been crippled by having weights dropped on their spines. They have been used in studies of organisms considered potential biological warfare agents; put into isolation rooms and sprayed with aerosol versions of the cholera bacterium, which kills through a ceaseless, draining diarrhea; injected with the Ebola virus, bringer of a hemorrhagic fever, which causes blood vessels to leak until a victim drowns in a rising tide of bloody fluid.

Deborah Blum, *The Monkey Wars.* New York: Oxford University Press, 1994.

Document 9: Trapping—Pain and Profit

The question of whether it is right to kill animals for their fur has generated heated debate in recent years. The People for the Ethical Treatment of Animals, an organization that has led the fight against fur, argues in the following section that the methods of capturing furbearing animals are inhumane.

The fur ads we see in magazines and commercials portray fur coats as a symbol of elegance. But these ads fail to show how the original owners of these coats met their gruesome deaths. Approximately 3.5 million furbearing animals—raccoons, coyotes, bobcats, lynxes, opossums, nutria, beavers, muskrats, otters, and others—are killed each year by trappers in the United States. Another 2.7 million animals are raised on fur "farms." Despite the fur industry's attempts to downplay the role of trapping in fur "production," it is estimated that more than half of all fur garments come from trapped animals.

Motives and Money

People trap for money and for "sport." In 1994, the International Association of Fish and Wildlife Agencies released a national survey indicating that just 4 percent of trappers' income is derived from trapping. Given the time investment of running a trap line, that 4 percent could be made up doing something that isn't cruel to animals. Amateur trappers kill animals in their spare time for fun and for additional income, although the average amateur earns only about $100 per trapping season.

Jaws and Paws

There are various types of traps, including snares, box traps, and cage traps, but the leghold trap is the most widely used. This simple but barbaric device has been banned in 63 countries, as well as in Florida, Rhode Island, New Jersey, and Arizona. The European Union banned the importation of furs from countries that use leghold traps on December 31, 1995. . . .

When an animal steps on the leghold trap spring, the trap's jaws slam on the animal's limb. Dr. Robert E. Cape explains that "if the trap is properly anchored, the captured animal will struggle to get loose, mutilating the foot and causing deep, painful lacerations. Or the animal will attempt escape by chewing or twisting off the trapped extremity. Ten to 12 hours after being captured, the animal is still in pain." After a prolonged time, he explains, trapped animals "will suffer from exhaustion, since they expend such a great amount of energy in attempting to escape. With exhaustion, the animal suffers from exposure, frostbite, shock, and eventually death."

It is estimated that up to one out of every four trapped animals escapes by chewing off his or her own foot. If these animals do not die from blood loss, infection, or gangrene, they will probably be killed by predators, hunters, or other traps. Victims of water-set traps, including beavers and muskrats, can take up to 20 agonizing minutes to drown.

Because many trapped animals are mutilated by predators before trappers return to claim their bodies, pole traps are often used. A pole trap is a form of leghold trap that is set in a tree or on a pole. Animals caught in these traps are hoisted into the air and left to hang by the caught appendage until they die or the trapper arrives to kill them.

The Fatal Finale

For animals who stay alive in the traps, further torture awaits them when the trappers return. State regulations on how often trappers must check their traps vary from 24 hours to one week, and four states have no regulations at all. Most state laws do not regulate the methods of slaughter for animals found alive in traps. To avoid damaging the pelt, trappers usually beat or stomp their victims to death. [According to writer Dan Dinello,] a common stomping method is "for the trapper to stand on the animal's rib cage, concentrating his weight near the heart. He then reaches down, takes the animal's hind legs in his hands, and yanks."

"Accidental" Victims

Every year hundreds of thousands of dogs, cats, birds, and other animals, including endangered species, are "accidentally" crippled or killed by traps. Trappers call these animals "trash kills" because they have no economic value.

Death and Disease

Contrary to fur industry propaganda, there is no ecologically sound reason to trap animals for "wildlife management." In fact, trapping disrupts wildlife populations by killing healthy animals needed to keep their species strong, and populations are further damaged when the parents of young animals are killed. Left alone, animal populations can and do regulate their own numbers. Even if human intervention or an unusual natural occurrence caused an animal population to rise temporarily, the group would soon stabilize through natural processes no more cruel, at their worst, than the pain and trauma of being trapped and slaughtered by humans. Killing animals because they might starve or might get sick is only an excuse for slaughter motivated by greed.

Another trapping side effect is the threat of rabies infection to both humans and wildlife. The spread of rabies including recent epidemics in the Eastern and Western U.S., has been directly linked to the interstate transport of infected "game" animals, especially raccoons and coyotes, by trappers trying to restock areas depleted by hunting and trapping.

Compassion and Fashion

In a 1992 survey of Arizona voters, 82 percent of the respondents agreed that "steel-jawed traps represent a cruel and inhumane method of taking wildlife." Trapping will become obsolete when people stop purchasing fur. You can discourage trapping by discouraging fur-wearing.

People for the Ethical Treatment of Animals, *PETA Factsheet: Trapping: Pain for Profit.*

Document 10: The Fur Industry's Take on Fur

The fur industry asserts that animal rights propaganda distorts the truth about fur. In the following section, which was taken from Fur Online's list of frequently asked questions about fur, the fur industry maintains that furbearing animals are treated humanely, regardless of whether they are raised on farms or trapped in the wild.

Which Furs Are Farm-Raised and Which Come From the Wild?

The vast majority of fur coats sold today come from animals raised on farms. In the United States, the figure is about eighty percent. Those coats are made of fox or mink—by far the best-selling fur. In addition, chinchilla, fitch, finnraccoon and nutria are raised in smaller numbers. The most popular wild animals used for fur coats are beaver, raccoon, muskrat, coyote, fox, nutria, lynx, fisher and even some mink.

Isn't It More Humane to Wear Furs that Are Farm-Raised?

Just as the choice to wear fur garments is a personal one, people sometimes have strong feelings about whether to wear farm-raised or wild-caught furs. Mink and foxes have been raised on farms since the turn of the century. Scandinavian countries produce the bulk of the world's farmed fur animals. Farms in several other countries raise fox and mink, and the U.S. is recognized for producing the finest quality mink in the world. Mink and fox have been called the world's best cared-for domestic animals, because any mistreatment would show up immediately on their pelts, devaluing them. Mink farmers have adopted codes of humane care that include regular visits by veterinarians.

Trapping furbearing animals is a wildlife conservation tool. In the U.S. and Canada, which produce the bulk of the international commercial fur trade's wild furs, the practice is exercised by government-licensed trappers and controlled by scientists. In Canada, indigenous humans living off the land still trap as part of their ancient heritage. Management of certain species will always be essential in a world where humans interact with wildlife habitat. Shrinking habitat due to human expansion is the biggest threat to most wild animals today. In fact, while hunting and trapping might be considered to be a threat to wild animal species, hunters and trappers actually provide the money—through licensing fees—used by government agencies to analyze and maintain those populations.

Living in finite habitats, wildlife populations left unmanaged frequently overpopulate. The results: they suffer starvation or become diseased (Mother Nature manages populations by spreading rabies, mange and other not-so-pretty afflictions); they infringe on human needs (damaging infrastructures, flooding roads, wandering into urban areas, sometimes dangerously coming into contact with small children); and even destroy their very own habitats (in Louisiana, overpopulated nutria are eating away valuable wetland areas). Therefore, man must intervene. Even when fur has no commercial value, trappers are sent to work, in some cases at taxpayer expense.

Does the Fur Trade Use Endangered Species?
Not at all! No reputable furrier sells garments made from endangered species. It is illegal. Poaching does continue in some parts of the world, but this is shameful and not condoned by any respectable furrier. The CITES Convention (Convention on International Trade in Endangered Species of Wild Fauna and Flora) is a world-wide body which determines which animals are endangered or threatened and then regulates their trade. Many of these animals cannot be imported, so they cannot even be obtained legally for sale. Others are strictly covered by quota schemes. . . .

Is Fur Politically Correct?
Most people these days are fed up with the dogma that is political correctness. Still, distinguish between its well-meaning original goals and its current, extremist-generated, twisted form. Animal rights activists equate the rights of rodents and chickens with the rights of women and many ethnic groups of people. This is odious to caring humans who strive to achieve a sensitivity to cultural differences, about which political correctness was meant to be. By definition, it sought inclusion, not intolerance. But it was twisted by fanatics. Animal rights activists—a group of people advocating a specific social agenda—represent a small minority of the world's population. Yet, like some religions, they continue to attempt to impose their viewpoints on society. This does not represent tolerance toward varying cultures but instead fascism. Witness only the attempt at genocide of Canada's native cultures, which are targets of animal rights activists because they live in harmony with the land and trap furbearing animals.

Furonline Factsheet, Winter 1995–96.

Document 11: The New Zoos

It has been said that zoos are poor environments for animals accustomed to the wild. Jared Diamond, however, describes the tactics contemporary zoos are developing to make zoo environments better substitutes for nature. The following section is excerpted from Diamond's article in the March 1995 issue of Discover *magazine.*

These days we take it for granted that we must provide for the physical and nutritional well-being of captive animals. Government and zoo-association inspectors regularly scrutinize zoos, and any institution that repeatedly lets its animals starve or become injured would be closed down. Now, at last, the U.S. Department of Agriculture and zoo professionals also expect zoos to provide for animals' psychological well-being. The key term is behavioral enrichment. That is, zoos are obligated to enrich an animal's environment in ways that permit it to engage in a variety of natural activities.

Behavioral enrichment assumes many forms to which nobody could possibly take offense. A few droplets of animal or plant scent essences can be placed around an otherwise monotonous exhibit to liven it up for its residents. Cats will rub against a scented object until they replace the foreign smell with their own. Bears like to shred raw cowhide, while big cats chew it, drag it around, roll on it, and try to bury it. Playing cassettes of natural sounds, including prey sounds, similarly elicits natural behavior.

An equally uncontroversial measure is to provide captive animals with the usual dead food but to make them use natural behavior to find it. The world's many small species of wild cats are considered unappealing zoo animals because they spend most of their time sleeping. Yet many small feline species are endangered in the wild and urgently need to be bred in zoos. An experiment on leopard cats, a species from India and southeastern Asia kept in the National Zoological Park in Washington, D.C., showed how easy it is to enrich these animals' lives.

Instead of leaving a pan of food once a day in the center of the exhibit, keepers divided the same food into four meals, which they brought at unpredictable times and hid around the display. With these simple changes in feeding procedures, the leopard cats spent less than half as much time at stereotyped pacing as they had before, interrupted their pacing bouts more often, and increased the time they spent exploring their exhibit threefold. They continued nosing around all day, even after they'd eaten the last bite, in hopes that there was still hidden food to be found.

Many other species respond well to similar gustatory challenges. Chimpanzees and bears, for example, love to pry or lick out raisins, blackberries, honey, or peanut butter stuffed into crannies or into holes drilled in logs; the chimps even use twigs to extract these treats, as they would in the wild. The caracal, an Asian and African cat that in the wild often leaps as high as 15 feet in the air to catch its prey, is happy to jump for its dinner when keepers hang food high in its exhibit.

Jared Diamond, "Playing God at the Zoo," *Discover,* March 1995.

Document 12: Dolphins in Captivity

In the following section, the Fund for Animals explains why it believes dolphins should not be held in captivity. According to animal rights organizations, a captive environment deprives dolphins of physical, mental, and emotional stimulation.

Because of their appeal and intelligence, dolphins have been used and abused for over 50 years by the military, in research facilities, and by the captive industry, which puts them in petting pools and swim-with programs.

More than 500 dolphins and other cetaceans are held in over 50 facilities in the U.S. today. The species which has shown to be the most adaptable and popular is the Atlantic bottlenose dolphin, although some 20 other species have been exhibited in limited numbers with less success. Between 1973 and 1988, 533 dolphins were captured; the majority (94%) of which were taken from coastal waters of the southeastern United States, an area including the Gulf of Mexico and Florida's Atlantic coast. At least 600 more were taken from Florida waters alone prior to the passage of the Marine Mammal Protection Act (MMPA) of 1972.

The practice of confining dolphins and other cetaceans has been highly criticized in recent years. Professor Hal Markowitz stated, "I know of no marine mammals kept in captivity in natural conditions. As a matter of fact, there is an inherent contradiction in using the term 'natural' to refer to captive circumstances." The greatest abuse suffered by dolphins is probably the *confinement* of these complex social animals, who are accustomed to swimming free in the open ocean with others of their own kind and choosing.

The absence of physical, mental, and emotional stimulation causes boredom and stress; the deprivation defies, depresses, and denies the instincts that define each animal. The captivity of cetaceans has become an issue of growing controversy, questioned by scientists, former trainers, government officials, and the general public. Heralded by the captive industry as "ambassadors of their species" through public relations rhetoric, not one individual has voluntarily abandoned its freedom and social status to be confined in barren concrete tanks of chemically treated, often manufactured, seawater, and fed unnatural diets.

Amendments to the MMPA in 1988 now require public display facilities to incorporate elements of education and conservation in their programs. This has presented facilities with a dilemma: an accurate depiction of the lives of dolphins could provoke a crusade against confinement, with the public demanding an end to captures, a halt to construction of new facilities, and a phasing out of public display. The workings of the industry are shrouded in secrecy, largely because the exploitation of dolphins and other cetaceans in aquariums and amusement parks depends on the public's belief that the animals are content in captivity.

Through advertising, performance, commentaries and guide books, aquariums have promoted the misconception that dolphins and other cetaceans are happy, care-free, friendly characters. Most marine parks are experienced in entertainment, not education. The animals are used as performers, in the circus tradition, and the performances reinforce the concept of human dominance over animals, while teaching nothing about the animals' own natural history or the concept of interspecies relationships. According to oceanographer Jacques Cousteau, captives represent an illusion of the species they represent, conditioned and deformed, bearing little resemblance to those living in the sea.

The social composite of coastal dolphin populations is generally comprised of females and calves, with the adult and sub-adult males forming separate groups. Adult males may form strong bonds in pairs or trios lasting up to ten years. Dominance hierarchies exist in the social structure of both wild and captive dolphins, with adult males dominant over all other tankmates. Adult males captured from the same groups have been maintained together with little aggression; yet when captive groupings contain adult males from different capture localities, the animals have been known to fight viciously over females or lead an injurious attack on a helpless poolmate. Therefore, most ocenaria now maintain a single adult male per tank.

Too little consideration has been given to the captive dolphin's *quality* of life. Bizarre and dangerous behavior patterns often occur. For example, one can only speculate why animals equipped with natural echolocation and sonic capabilities have collided with pool walls, with resulting injury and even death.

Aquariums can and do provide valuable educational opportunities *without* confining dolphins and other cetaceans. Many existing and proposed facilities have decided *not* to exhibit any cetacean species. Marine mammal authority Stephen Leatherwood stated, "We as a culture may soon decide that marine zoological parks and aquariums are outmoded, that the kind of education presented in them can be offered by other means. Considering the many human pressures on the wild environment today, the additional stress of capturing animals from the wild for display may no longer be tolerable."

Fund for Animals, "Dolphins in Captivity," http://www.fund.org/facts/dolphins.html.

APPENDIX B

Facts About Animal Rights

—According to 1995 statistics, approximately 35.8 million cows, 1.5 million veal calves, 4.6 million sheep and lambs, 96.5 million hogs, and 7.5 billion chickens are slaughtered each year in the United States.

—Of the animals used in laboratory tests, 90 percent are rodents, 1.5 percent are dogs and cats, 0.5 percent are primates, and the remaining 8 percent are other animals.

—Roughly 1,500 chimpanzees live in American research institutions.

—According to statistics by the United States Department of Agriculture, 54 percent of animal experiments involved no pain or distress, 35 percent used anesthesia to alleviate pain, and 11 percent involved pain yet used no anesthetics.

—Approximately 9 percent of the American population hunts.

—The top five hunting states are Wyoming, Montana, Idaho, South Dakota, and Vermont.

—According to the U.S. Fish and Wildlife Service and the Wildlife Legislative Fund of America, 43 percent of U.S. hunters hunt for sport, 25 percent hunt for food, 21 percent hunt to be close to nature, and 12 percent hunt to be with family and friends.

—The number of hunting licenses sold in the U.S. fell from 16.7 million in 1982 to 15.2 million in 1995.

STUDY QUESTIONS

Chapter 1

1. According to Viewpoint 1, why is lack of intelligence an insufficient reason to deny rights to animals? What is the main reason cited in Viewpoint 1 for why animals have rights? Do you find this reason convincing?

2. Explain the term *speciesism*. According to Viewpoint 1, why is speciesism wrong? What support does Viewpoint 2 provide for the opposite view?

3. R.G. Frey argues in Viewpoint 2 that human lives are more valuable than animal lives because human existence is made up of activities, goals, and desires that are not accessible to animals. Do you agree with Frey's contention that animals are less valuable than humans? Explain your answer.

Chapter 2

1. List the arguments in Viewpoint 2 in favor of vegetarianism. Which, if any, of these do you find persuasive and why?

2. In Viewpoint 1, Stephen Bodio defends meat-eating on the grounds that meat tastes delicious. Is this sufficient justification for eating meat, in your opinion?

3. On what basis does Viewpoint 2 contend that eating meat is unhealthy? How does Viewpoint 1 refute that claim?

4. According to Viewpoint 2, the drive to produce more meat in less time results in animals being neglected or abused. On the other hand, Viewpoint 1 argues that the meat industry treats animals well in order to ensure a high quality of meat. Which argument do you feel is closer to the truth and why?

Chapter 3

1. What evidence does Viewpoint 1 provide to support the idea that animal experimentation is essential to medical progress? What evidence does Viewpoint 2 offer contradicting that position?

2. According to Viewpoint 2, why is it always wrong to use animals in medical experiments? What other argument against vivisection is provided by Viewpoint 2?

3. Viewpoint 3 claims to offer a middle-ground position on the use of animals in medical research. Describe the position outlined in Viewpoint 3. According to this viewpoint, when is it appropriate to use animals in medical research? When is it not appropriate?

Chapter 4

1. List and briefly describe the hunting practices mentioned in Viewpoint 1. In your view, are these practices unethical? Why or why not?

2. According to Viewpoint 1, who has the advantage in a match between a hunter and an animal? Why?

3. In Viewpoint 2, Gene Mueller contends that a person who eats meat cannot logically oppose hunting. Do you agree with his position? Explain your views.

4. In Viewpoint 3, on what basis does Jared Diamond assert that zoos are not good environments for animals?

5. According to Viewpoint 3, are zoos educational? Why or why not?

6. Describe captive breeding programs, as mentioned in Viewpoint 4. What evidence does Viewpoint 4 give in favor of captive breeding programs? How does Viewpoint 3 refute this position?

7. According to Michael H. Robinson in Viewpoint 4, why are zoos the most effective way to preserve endangered species? Do you agree with his view?

ORGANIZATIONS TO CONTACT

The editors have compiled the following list of organizations concerned with the issues debated in this book. The descriptions are derived from materials provided by the organizations. All have publications or information available for interested readers. The list was compiled on the date of publication of the present volume; the information provided here may change. Be aware that many organizations take several weeks or longer to respond to inquiries, so allow as much time as possible.

American Anti-Vivisection Society (AAVS)
801 Old York Rd., Suite 204
Jenkintown, PA 19046-1685
(215) 887-0816 • fax: (215) 887-2088
web address: http://www.aavs.org

AAVS advocates the abolition of vivisection, opposes all types of experiments on living animals, and sponsors research on alternatives to these methods. The society produces videos and publishes numerous brochures, including *Problems with Product Testing* and the *Student Guide to Saving Animals*.

American Association for Laboratory Animal Science (AALAS)
70 Timber Creek Dr.
Cordova, TN 38018
(901) 754-8620 • fax: (901) 753-0046
e-mail: info@aalas.org • web address: http://www.aalas.org

AALAS collects and exchanges information on all aspects of management, care, and procurement of laboratory animals. Its publications include *Contemporary Topics in Laboratory Animal Science and Laboratory Animal Science.*

American Society for the Prevention of Cruelty to Animals (ASPCA)
424 E. 92nd St.
New York, NY 10128-6804
(212) 876-7700 • fax: (212) 348-3031
e-mail: press@aspca.org • web address: http://www.aspca.org

The ASPCA promotes appreciation for and humane treatment of animals, encourages enforcement of anticruelty laws, and works for the passage of legislation that strengthens existing animal protection laws. In addition to making available books, brochures, and videos on animal issues, the ASPCA publishes *Animal Watch*, a quarterly magazine.

American Zoo and Aquarium Association (AZA)
7970-D Old Georgetown Rd.
Bethesda, MD 20814

(301) 907-7777 • fax: (301) 907-2980

web address: http://www.aza.org

AZA represents over 160 zoos and aquariums in North America. The association provides information on captive breeding of endangered species, conservation education, natural history, and wildlife legislation. AZA publications include the *Species Survival Plans* and the *Annual Report on Conservation and Science*. Both publications are available from the Office of Membership Services, Oglebay Park, Wheeling, WV 26003-1698.

Farm Animal Reform Movement (FARM)

PO Box 30654

Bethesda, MD 20824

(301) 530-1737

e-mail: farm@farmusa.org • web address: http://www.farmusa.org

FARM seeks to moderate and eliminate animal suffering and other adverse impacts of commercial animal production. It promotes the annual observance of March 20 as the "Great American Meatout," a day of meatless meals, and provides a variety of brochures and fact sheets for consumers and activists.

Foundation for Biomedical Research (FBR)

818 Connecticut Ave. NW, Suite 303

Washington, DC 20006

(202) 457-0654 • fax: (202) 457-0659

e-mail: info@fbresearch.org • web address: http://www.fbresearch.org

FBR provides information and educational programs about the necessary and important role of laboratory animals in biomedical research and testing. Its videos include *The New Research Environment* and *Caring for Life*. It also publishes the brochures *Animal Research for Animal Health* and *Animal Research: Fact vs. Myth*.

Humane Society of the United States (HSUS)

2100 L St. NW

Washington, DC 20037

(202) 452-1100 • fax: (202) 778-6132

web address: http://www.hsus.org

HSUS works to foster respect, understanding, and compassion for all creatures. Among its many diverse efforts, it maintains programs supporting responsible pet ownership and the elimination of cruelty in hunting and trapping. It also exposes painful uses of animals in research and testing and abusive treatment of animals in movies, circuses, pulling contests, and racing. It campaigns for animal protection legislation and monitors the enforcement of existing animal protection statutes. HSUS publishes the quarterlies *Animal Activist Alert* and *HSUS News*.

National Cattlemen's Association (NCA)
1301 Pennsylvania Ave. NW, Suite 300
Washington, DC 20004
(202) 347-0228 • fax: (202) 638-0607
e-mail: cows@beef.org • web address: http://www.beef.org/ncba.htm

NCA functions as the central agency for national public information on beef and acts as the legislative and industry liaison for farmers, ranchers, breeders, and feeders of beef cattle. It publishes the monthly *National Cattlemen* and the weekly *Beef Business Bulletin*.

People for the Ethical Treatment of Animals (PETA)
501 Front St.
Norfolk, VA 23510
(757) 622-PETA (7382) • fax: (757) 622-0457
e-mail: peta@norfolk.infi.net • web address: http://www.peta-online. org

An international animal rights organization, PETA is dedicated to establishing and protecting the rights of all animals. It focuses on four areas: factory farms, research laboratories, the fur trade, and the entertainment industry. PETA promotes public education, cruelty investigations, animal rescue, celebrity involvement, and legislative action. It produces numerous videos and publishes the children's magazine *Animal Times, Grrr!* as well as various fact sheets, brochures, and flyers.

U.S. Fish and Wildlife Service
e-mail: web_reply@fws.gov • web address: http://www.fws.gov/

The U.S. Fish and Wildlife Service is a network of regional offices, national wildlife refuges, research and development centers, national fish hatcheries, and wildlife law enforcement agents. The service's primary goal is to conserve, protect, and enhance fish and wildlife and their habitats. It publishes fact sheets, pamphlets, and information on the Endangered Species Act.

Vegetarian Resource Group (VRG)
PO Box 1463
Baltimore, MD 21203
(410) 366-VEGE (8343)
e-mail: vrg@vrg.org • web address: http://www.vrg.org

VRG membership is primarily made up of health professionals, activists, and educators working with businesses and individuals to bring about healthy nutritional changes in schools, workplaces, and communities. It educates the public about vegetarianism and veganism and examines vegetarian issues as they relate to good health, animal rights, ethics, world hunger, and ecology. VRG publishes books on vegetarianism, a computer software game, and the bimonthly newsletter *Vegetarian Journal*.

FOR FURTHER READING

Deborah Blum, *The Monkey Wars*. New York: Oxford University Press, 1994. This book is an account of the author's tour of primate research centers throughout the country. She reports her experience clearly and vividly, with an unbiased eye.

Michael Allen Fox, *The Case for Animal Experimentation*. Berkeley and Los Angeles: University of California Press, 1986. In his detailed argument in favor of animal experimentation, Fox addresses ethical and scientific questions. The book offers a complex analysis of why animals do not have rights.

Gary L. Francione, *Rain Without Thunder: The Ideology of the Animal Rights Movement*. Philadelphia: Temple University Press, 1996. The author provides a theoretical analysis of the animal rights movement and its philosophy. The book deals with topics such as the origins of the animal rights movement, the difference between animal welfare and animal rights, and whether animal rights is a "utopian" theory.

Lorenz Otto Lutherer and Margaret Sheffield Simon, *The Anatomy of an Animal Rights Attack*. Norman: University of Oklahoma Press, 1992. The authors of this book discuss an animal rights raid on Texas Tech University. The book defends the use of animals in research and condemns animals rights activists for their violent tactics.

Jim Mason, *An Unnatural Order: Uncovering the Roots of Our Domination of Nature and Each Other*. New York: Simon & Schuster, 1993. This book provides a fascinating look at the roots of human domination over nature and animals and how this domination has led to environmental and moral decay. The author writes on a fairly high level.

Charles D. Niven, *History of the Humane Movement*. London: Johnson, 1967. This book catalogs the history of the humane movement and discusses key events in the struggle against animal cruelty.

F. Barbara Orlans, *In the Name of Science: Issues in Responsible Animal Experimentation*. New York: Oxford University Press, 1993. Orlans argues that limits should be set in regard to the use of animals in medical research. She discusses the history of animal experimentation, relevant legislation, the benefits of animal research, alternative methods to animal experimentation, and ethical questions about subjecting animals to pain.

Tom Regan, *The Struggle for Animal Rights*. Clarks Summit, PA: International Society for Animal Rights, 1987. The essays collected in this book represent Regan's informal writing on the subject of animal rights. The book is conversational in tone and easy to read.

Tom Regan and Peter Singer, eds., *Animal Rights and Human Obligations*. New Jersey: Prentice-Hall, 1989. This book is a collection of short essays whose authors include ancient Greek philosopher Aristotle, René Descartes, Charles Darwin, Voltaire, and modern-day animal rights philosophers Peter Singer and Tom Regan. The book provides contrasting views on animal experimentation, factory farming, and other issues related to animal rights. Although the text focuses on philosophical issues, it is still appropriate for beginning animal rights scholars.

Henry S. Salt, *Animals' Rights*. 1892. Reprint, Clarks Summit, PA: Society for Animal Rights, 1980. Written in 1892, this book presents one of the first detailed arguments in favor of animal rights.

Upton Sinclair, *The Jungle*. 1906. Reprint, Urbana and Chicago: University of Illinois Press, 1988. This book exposes the inner workings of Chicago slaughterhouses in the early 1900s. Sinclair's horrific tale of the filthy conditions in American meat processing led to the passage of the 1906 Pure Food and Drug Act. While the book was intended to call attention to the plight of the Chicago working class, Sinclair's descriptions of meat processing incited many people to vegetarianism.

WORKS CONSULTED

Books

Jeremy Bentham, *Introduction to the Principles of Morals and Legislation.* 1780. Reprint, New York: Hafner Press, 1948. Written in 1780, this book contains a brief passage in which Bentham defends the rights of animals. Bentham was one of the first philosophers to argue in favor of animal rights on the basis that animals, like humans, are sentient beings who experience pain.

Charles Darwin, *Life and Letters of Charles Darwin.* New York: BasicBooks, 1959. In his letters Charles Darwin discusses his theory of evolution, his views on species differences, and other issues.

Lawrence Finsen and Susan Finsen, *The Animal Rights Movement in America: From Compassion to Respect.* New York: Twayne, 1994. The authors provide a readable and detailed history of the animal rights movement.

Michael W. Fox, *Animals Have Rights, Too.* New York: Continuum, 1991. Fox presents simple and straightforward arguments in favor of animal rights.

Jane Goodall, *Through a Window: My Thirty Years with the Chimpanzees of Gombe.* Boston: Houghton Mifflin, 1990. This book is an eloquent tale of Goodall's experience working with chimpanzees.

Andrew Harnack, ed., *Animal Rights: Opposing Viewpoints.* San Diego: Greenhaven Press, 1996. This book presents contrasting views on animal rights issues such as animal experimentation, vegetarianism, hunting, zoos, and the genetic engineering of farm animals. Though it provides some in-depth discussion of animal rights philosophy, the book is straightforward and understandable.

James M. Jasper and Dorothy Nelkin, *The Animal Rights Crusade: The Growth of a Moral Protest.* New York: Free Press, 1992. The authors, who are advocates of animal rights, provide a clear, comprehensive account of the origins of the animal rights movement.

Rush H. Limbaugh, *The Way Things Ought to Be.* New York: Simon & Schuster, 1992. This book contains a chapter in which Limbaugh argues against the notion that animals have rights. The chapter is humorous and easy to understand.

Harriet Ritvo, *The Animal Estate*. Cambridge, MA: Harvard University Press, 1987. This enjoyable book discusses the role of animals in Victorian England. It deals with issues such as the early antivivisection movement, zoology, hunting, and pet ownership.

Richard D. Ryder, *Animal Revolution*. Oxford: Basil Blackwell, 1989. This book provides an overview of the animal welfare and animal rights movements.

Peter Singer, *Animal Liberation*. New York: New York Review of Books, 1990. In this book, which has frequently been called "the bible" of the animal rights movement, Singer presents a philosophical defense of animal rights. Singer's argument, unlike many others, is intellectual, not emotional. The book is challenging and extremely thought-provoking.

Periodicals

American Association for Laboratory Animal Science, "Use of Animals in Biomedical Research: Understanding the Issues," undated pamphlet.

Don Barnes, "Vivisection: A Window to the Dark Ages of Science," *Animals' Agenda*, July/August 1996.

Gene Bauston, "For a Mouthful of Flesh," *Animals' Agenda*, March 1998.

Tom L. Beauchamp, "Why Treat the Human Animal Differently?" *World & I*, April 1995.

Christine Bertelson, "With $40 Million, Zoo Should Save the Real Thing," *St. Louis Post-Dispatch*, November 16, 1995.

Stephen Bodio, "Strange Meat," *Northern Lights*, May 1996.

Tom Brakefield, "A Short History of Zoos," *Lamp*, Winter 1995/1996.

Andrew Breslin, "Non-Animal Methods Triumph in AIDS Research," *Anti-Vivisection Magazine*, Spring 1997.

Lonny J. Brown, "Ethical Pest Control," *Yoga Journal*, June 1995.

Peggy Carlson, "Whose Health Is It, Anyway?" *Animals' Agenda*, November/December 1996.

Lawrence Carter-Long, "Life Without Mother," *Mainstream*, Winter 1997.

Ann S. Causey, "What's the Problem with Hunting?" *Orion*, Winter 1996.

Stephen R.L. Clark, "Conservation and Animal Welfare," *Chronicles*, June 1996.

Merritt Clifton, "Life on the Farm Isn't Very Laid Back," *Animal People*, October 1995.

Gail Collins, "Cook the Geese: A Good Word for Bambi-Bashing," *New York Times*, October 6, 1996.

Julianne Couch and Tracey Rembert, "Back from the Brink," *E: the Environmental Magazine*, July/August 1996.

Geoffrey Cowley and Adam Rogers, "Of Mice and Men," *Newsweek*, May 18, 1998.

Jared Diamond, "Playing God at the Zoo," *Discover*, March 1995.

"Fact Sheet: What's Wrong with Trapping?" *Trans-Species Unlimited*.

Camilla Fox, "What Trappers Won't Tell You," *Mainstream*, Fall 1997.

Egypt Freeman, "The Meat of the Matter," *Health Quest*, February 28, 1995.

R.G. Frey, "Medicine and the Ethics of Animal Experimentation," *World & I*, April 1995.

———, "Moral Standing, the Value of Lives, and Speciesism," *Between the Species*, Summer 1988.

Maneka Gandhi, "Animal Welfare Is Human Welfare," *Resurgence*, March/April 1996.

Dallas Glenn, "In Defense of Animal Consciousness," *Animals' Voice Magazine*, Spring 1996.

John P. Gluck, "Has Anything Really Changed?" *AV Magazine*, Winter 1998.

Temple Grandin, "How to Think Like an Animal," *Utne Reader*, March/April 1998.

Charles Hirshberg, "Miracle Babies," *Life*, March 1997.

David Hubel, "Animal Rights Movement Threatens Progress of U.S. Medical Research," *Scientist*, November 15, 1993.

"Hunting Restrictions," *Issues and Controversies On File*, February 7, 1997.

Morton A. Kaplan, "A Different Position on Animal Rights," *World & I*, April 1995.

Ryland Loos, "Friends of the Hunted," *Conservationist*, November 1993.

Howard Lyman, "Confessions of a 'Vegan' Cattle Rancher," *Perceptions*, March/April 1996.

Wendy Marston, "Beef Makes a Comeback," *Health*, November/December 1996.

David Masci, "Fighting over Animal Rights," *CQ Researcher*, August 2, 1996.

Colman McCarthy, "Vegetarian Diets Are Healthy," *Liberal Opinion*, January 22, 1996.

Terry McDonell, "Hunters Are Not Gun Nuts," *New York Times*, June 3, 1995.

Gene Mueller, "Why Modern Men (and, Increasingly, Women) Hunt," *Washington Times*, September 20, 1996.

Eileen Murphy, "Zoos and Endangered Species: A Special Report," *Vegetarian*, February 1993.

Joseph E. Murray, "Animals Hold the Key to Saving Human Lives," *Los Angeles Times*, February 5, 1996.

National Anti-Vivisection Society, "The Truth About Cancer Research," *Expressions 2*, 1994.

————, "The Ugly Side of the Beauty Business," *Expressions 2*, 1994.

"New Healthy Diet Pyramid Emphasizes Vegetarian Eating," *Business Wire*, November 26, 1997.

Geoffrey Norman, "Death in Venison," *American Spectator*, Fall 1997.

Charley Reese, "Animal Welfare vs. Animal Rights," *Conservative Chronicle*, January 24, 1996.

Robert Rich, "Red Tape Strangles Animal-Based Research," *Wall Street Journal*, August 29, 1995.

Jeremy Rifkin, "The Deconstruction of Modern Meat," *Orion*, Winter 1996.

Michael H. Robinson, "Beyond the Ark," *Issues in Science and Technology*, Spring 1993.

Richard Ryder, "Toward Kinship: Speciesism and 'Painism,'" *Animals' Agenda*, January/February 1997.

Heloisa Sabin, "Animal Research Saves Human Lives," *Wall Street Journal*, October 18, 1995.

Karen Singer, "The Inner Life of Animals," *E: the Environmental Magazine*, September/October 1995.

Michael Sissons, "The Wrongs of Animal Rights," *Spectator*, September 2, 1995.

James P. Skelly, "Animal Rights and Human Needs," *American Atheist*, June 1989.

Henry Spira, "Less Meat, Less Misery: Reforming Factory Farms," *Forum for Applied Research and Public Policy*, Spring 1996.

Ike C. Sugg, "Animal Rights, Exotic Bans," *CEI Update*, March 1996.

Colin Tudge, "Better Captive Than Dead," *Independent on Sunday*, October 13, 1996.

Dan Wharton, "Zoo Breeding Efforts: An Ark of Survival?" *Forum for Applied Research and Public Policy*, Spring 1995.

Aaron Wildavsky, "Regulation of Carcinogens: Are Animal Tests a Sound Foundation?" *Independent Review*, Spring 1996.

Joy Williams, "The Inhumanity of the Animal People," *Harper's*, August 1997.

Electronic Sources

American Meat Institute, "Just the Facts." Accessed July 17, 1998. On-line. Internet. Available http://www.meatami.org.

Americans for Medical Progress Educational Foundation, "Without Animal Research." Accessed September 24, 1998. On-line. Internet. Available http://www.ampef.org/research.htm.

Fund for Animals, "Dolphins in Captivity." Accessed July 17, 1998. On-line. Internet. Available http://www.fund.org/facts/dolphins.html.

Fur Online, "FAQ and Quotes," Winter 1995–96. Accessed July 16, 1998. On-line. Internet. Available http://www.furs.com/faq.html.

People for the Ethical Treatment of Animals, "Alternatives: Testing Without Torture." Accessed July 16, 1998. On-line. Internet. Available http://www.peta-online.org/facts/exp/fsex08.htm.

———, "Trapping: Pain for Profit." Accessed July 16, 1998. On-line. Internet. Available http://www.peta-online.org/facts/wil/fswil02.htm.

———, "Zoos: Pitiful Prisons." Accessed July 16, 1998. On-line. Internet. Available http:// www.peta-online.org/facts.

Spiritual Realization Institute, "The Real Cost of Beef." Accessed July 17, 1998. On-line. Internet. Available http://www.neonblue.com/sri/suffer.htm.

U.S. Dept. of Agriculture, Animal and Plant Health Inspection Service, "APHIS Factsheet," March 1995. Accessed July 16, 1998. On-line. Internet. Available http://www.aphis.usda.gov/reac/awa.html.

INDEX

aflatoxin, 51
AIDS, 44–45, 51
American Antivivisection Society, 12, 98
American Association for Laboratory Animal Science, 46, 98
American Dietetic Association Journal, 40
American Fund for Alternatives to Animal Research, 14
American Meat Institute, 35
Americans for Medical Progress Educational Foundation, 18
American Society for the Prevention of Cruelty to Animals (ASPCA), 12, 14, 98
angiogenesis inhibitors, 56–57
angiostatin, 57
Animal Liberation (Singer), 15, 25
Animal Minds (Griffin), 22
Animal Rights International, 38
animals
  are human prey, 66
  are incapable of moral action, 29
  are not as valuable as humans, 27
  are vicious, 29–30, 36
  in captivity, 68–69
  in circuses, 69
  cute versus ugly, 64
  electrical stunning of, 38–39
  exist to benefit humans, 18–19, 25, 30, 44, 63–64
  experimentation
    in AIDS research, 44–45, 51
    alternatives to, 52
    brings medical advances, 17–18, 43–46
    in Britain, 57
    can be useful, 54, 56–57
    in cancer research, 50–51, 56–57
    does not bring medical advances, 48–52
    history of, 10–12
    horrors of, 48
    and humane societies, 11–13
    is unreliable, 49–51
    should end, 16–17

useless tests in, 55–56
  as "exploited" class, 25–26, 30–31, 70
  feel pain, 14–15, 24, 26, 59–60
  grain consumption of, 40
  habitats of, 70, 73
  hunted for food, 18, 63
  intelligence of, 22–24, 29
  protected by laws, 8–10, 13–14, 16
  rights, 19, 22–24
    activists for, 14–17, 18–19
    are obsessed with victimhood, 30–31
    on medical research, 45
    protest tests on animals, 23, 43, 44
    for cute animals, 64
    in England, 8–10
    opponents of, 22, 26, 27, 29
    speciesism of, 24–25, 30
    restrict medical research, 44–45
    violations of, 22, 48
  treatment of
    in meatpacking plants, 35–36, 37
    in medical research, 14, 54–55
    when raised for food, 37–39
Animals' Agenda, 16
Animal Welfare Act, 14
antivivisectionist groups, 12, 49, 54, 98
AV Magazine, 51
AZT, 51

baiting, 59
Barnes, Don, 49
bears, 59
Beauchamp, Tom L., 22
beef. *See* meat consumption
Beef Industry Council, 33
Bertelson, Christine, 70
Beyond Beef: The Rise and Fall of the Cattle Culture (Rifken), 37
Bible, 18, 25, 30
Bodio, Stephen, 33–34
breeding. *See* captive breeding
Breslin, Andrew, 51
Bross, Irwin D.J., 50

ABOUT THE AUTHOR

Jennifer Hurley is a series editor for Greenhaven Press and also writes fiction. She has worked as a ghostwriter, taught freshman composition, and attended graduate school at Boston University, where she received an M.A. in creative writing. She currently resides in San Diego.